Over **150** Essential
Jigs, Aids
& Devices

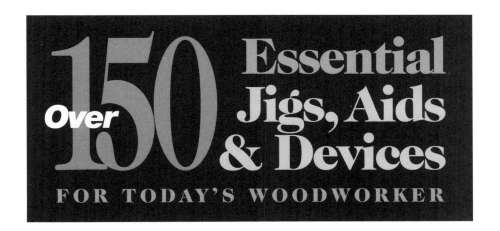

Over 150 Essential Jigs, Aids & Devices

FOR TODAY'S WOODWORKER

V. J. TAYLOR

David & Charles

A DAVID & CHARLES BOOK

First published in the UK in 1998

A catalogue record for this book is available from the British Library.

ISBN 0 7153 0686 3

Designed by Paul Cooper
and printed in Italy by LEGO SpA, Vincenza
for David & Charles
Brunel House   Newton Abbot   Devon

CONTENTS

ACKNOWLEDGEMENTS

This book is dedicated to my wife, with thanks for her word-processing skills! My thanks are due also to my friend and neighbour, David Beard, who took time off from his woodturning to help me with the 'hands-on' work for the router jigs in Chapter 4, as I was unable to do it myself because of illness.

INTRODUCTION

Increased leisure and early retirement have meant that in recent years many people have taken up woodworking as a rewarding hobby – and most have found that they like the tactile 'feel' of wood and are pleasantly stimulated by the challenge to create something unique about which they can truly say 'I made it myself'.

Few woodworkers are fortunate enough to be able to set up an ideal workshop from scratch. Most of us simply have to make the best of what we have and this book begins by looking at ways in which to do this, providing hints and suggestions on aspects such as insulation, electrical matters, rust prevention and safety requirements.

There is no doubt that the costs of setting yourself up with even basic tools and equipment can quickly mount up, especially with the advent of man-made particle boards such as blockboards, chipboards and, most importantly, medium density fibreboards (MDF), which have now supplanted hardwoods as the first choice for building cabinet furniture. MDF, in particular, is so versatile and responds so well to being machined that it can be said to have ushered in an era of 'wood engineering' rather than 'woodwork' – with a corresponding rise in the cost of setting up a home workshop complete with the necessary machines. Important sections of the book therefore explain the characteristics of softwoods, hardwoods and man-made boards and appropriate ways in which to use them, and then discuss the specifications and potentials of a wide range of workshop machines, pointing out the pros and cons of each so that you can decide which will best fulfil your woodworking needs.

Every woodworker is interested in aids and accessories which can guarantee near-perfect results or greatly increase the scope of their machines and equipment – frequently saving them money at the same time – and a vast array of jigs and devices designed to do just that are described and illustrated in detail. A good example of this approach is the power router, which has a chapter all to itself. Here is a basic machine which, when combined with the appropriate jigs and accessories, can undertake dovetailing, joint-cutting, rebating, grooving, and shaping mouldings – a truly versatile performer!

Nevertheless, hand tools also have an important part to play, and those still worthy of a place in the workshop today are described in full, along with techniques and tips for using and sharpening them, plus a wide range of jigs and accessories for use in hand work.

Woodturning is a popular 'hands-on' craft in its own right, and some useful devices that can make the work easier are included in a chapter that also covers woodwork-related subjects such as veneering and wood finishing.

Finally, techniques for measuring and marking accurately – essential for producing professional-looking results – and all the most common technical terms the home woodworker is likely to encounter are explained in detail, to complete a book that I hope will become an essential reference manual to be kept within easy reach in every workshop. Armed with the information contained within it, woodworkers will be able to refine and enhance not only the craft skills of their own hands but also the effectiveness of their tools and equipment.

Chapter *1*

THE WORKSHOP

When setting up a workshop, the first consideration is, of course, its location. In fact, most woodworkers have little choice in the matter and have to settle for either sharing the garage with the car or fitting up a wooden shed in the garden. Those who can afford to have a custom-built workshop tailored to their requirements are in the minority and do not need any help from us!

If you are setting up a workshop in your garage, this will mean that the car has to stand outside while woodworking is in progress, but for most people this is an acceptable option. The bonuses are that electricity will be available for light, heat and power, and the building should already be weatherproof. It is not until you have to use the workshop over several evenings when the weather is bitterly cold and wet that you will begin to appreciate that the garage can be lit and heated at the flick of a switch: compare this with sliding down a sodden grass path to an unheated shed that is wet and damp – and feels it!

In both cases, you will need insulation against noise (for your neighbours' benefit), and against loss of heat (for your own) to avoid the all-too-common situation where the workshop only becomes bearable when it's time to switch off the lights and go indoors. You will also need to take steps to control the ravages of rust among your precious tools and equipment.

INSULATING AGAINST NOISE

If you live in a built-up area (as most of us do), you will need to make sure that your woodworking is not so noisy as to annoy the neighbours. If you ignore this common courtesy, you may find yourself subject to a visit from the local authority and compelled to take some pretty drastic measures. There are several ways to keep noise to a minimum, many of which involve changes to the doors and windows of your workshop, as it is through these that a lot of noise can escape.

Fitting ordinary draughtproofing seals all around the doors will help, as they will not only prevent some noise from escaping but will also damp down any vibration the doors themselves may transmit. You could line them inside by pinning on panels of insulation board, which will make the doors thicker and less likely to transmit sound, but check that the hinges can carry the extra weight.

Windows can also be sealed with draughtproofing tape and fitted with secondary glazing consisting of, say, 6mm (¼in) thick glass fixed in a frame which will hold it about 19mm (¾in) away from the glass of the window; to prevent condensation from forming in the space, use a hair-drier or something similar to blow warm dry air over the frame while you are fixing the glass. This ensures that the air space contains only dry air and so condensation cannot form from any trapped moisture.

Fig 1 shows an effective way to insulate walls by lining them with plasterboard pinned to studs, which in turn are fixed to the walls; the intervening space is filled with the kind of mineral- or glass-fibre quilt used for roof insulation. Indeed, the same process can be used to

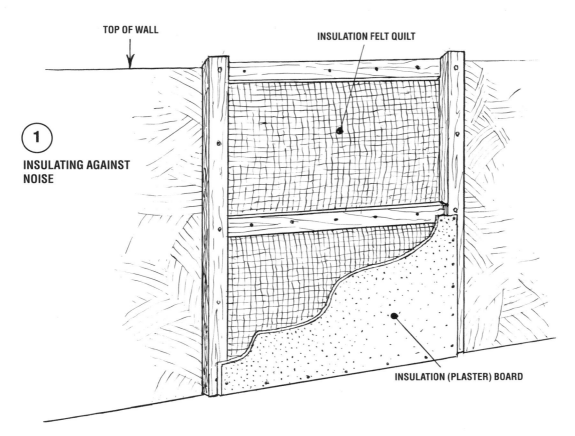

TOP OF WALL

INSULATION FELT QUILT

1

INSULATING AGAINST NOISE

INSULATION (PLASTER) BOARD

insulate the roof, provided that the timbers are strong enough to take the extra weight.

All these methods of insulation greatly reduce the air flow and it is essential that fresh air should be introduced somehow. This could be by means of fans, by introducing air bricks into masonry walls or, in a wooden shed, by using hit-or-miss ventilators.

Make sure that your bench, and any machine which is particularly noisy, is not attached to the wall or any part of the work-

shop structure, otherwise the noise and vibration it makes can be transmitted through to the outside. It also helps if you can carry out noisy jobs away from doors and windows whenever possible.

Finally, don't forget you only get one pair of ears, so it makes sense to buy yourself a pair of ear muffs or defenders, or a set or two of earplugs. The muffs or defenders should carry the British Standard kite mark and be tested to BS6344.

INSULATING FOR WARMTH

Whether your workshop is in the garage or a shed in the garden, the problem of heating it and then retaining that heat is the same and is best solved by installing some form of insulation. Luckily, the same method can be employed in both situations. It is illustrated in **fig 2**, where it is applied to a shed that has the usual wood-cladding walls consisting of either tongued and grooved or shiplap boards, but it would be equally effective on the walls of a garage.

The first step is to fix lengths of 50 x 50mm (2 x 2in) softwood to the inside of the walls. These are called 'studs' and reach from floor to ceiling; the horizontal pieces, which are the same thickness and are fixed between the studs to add strength, are called 'noggins'. Sheets of damp-resistant builder's paper are interposed between the studs and noggins and the walls, and are held in place by fixings. On a garage wall these will be screws and wall plugs, and on a wooden shed they will be screws driven in from outside.

You will now need some cavity wall 'batts' of the kind used by builders between the inner and outer walls of a house. They are made from

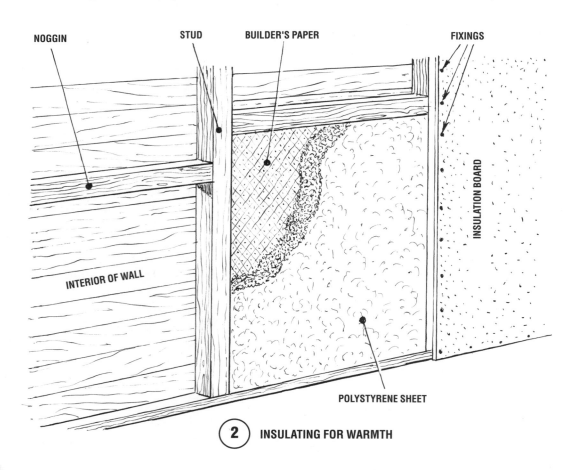

NOGGIN   STUD   BUILDER'S PAPER   FIXINGS

INSULATION BOARD

INTERIOR OF WALL

POLYSTYRENE SHEET

2 INSULATING FOR WARMTH

polystyrene insulating material, which is also often used for packing, and come in 2440 x 1220mm (8 x 4ft) sheets in a range of thicknesses: 50mm (2in) is the one to use. The polystyrene is easily cut with a sharp knife or, best of all, an electric carving knife, but be warned – as you cut you will be showered with hundreds of tiny white balls which stick to *everything*, so keep a vacuum cleaner handy. Most of the polystyrene sheet can be wedged in place, but any loose pieces are best stuck down with strips of double-sided adhesive tape or the special adhesive used to stick polystyrene ceiling tiles. The latter can, of course, be used to insulate the underside of the roof.

Finally, you will need to choose and fix the internal cladding. Hardboard is cheap, readily available and no problem to cut and fix with hardboard pins, but it is not strong enough to act as a fixing for hooks, shelves, racks and the like, while a thicker, stronger insulation board which is more expensive will act as a good anchorage for these fittings. In either case, the boards should be cut into panels that butt against each other along the centre lines of the studs and noggins, so that each board is fastened around the edges.

The finish you use is, of course, up to you, but it is worth covering all the panel joints with cover strips, which need only be strips of hardboard about 25mm (1in) wide; if at any future time you want to make alterations or install electrical cables, the strips will show you where the existing fixings are.

RUST PREVENTION

Even if your workshop has been fully insulated against heat loss, you may still have to contend with rust attacking your tools gradually, although it is never likely to be so bad as to make them useless, but merely unsightly.

The method used to heat the workshop is one of the main factors in rust prevention. Both gas and paraffin heaters produce appreciable amounts of moisture and only some form of electrical heating can be guaranteed to supply dry heat. If you are in the workshop day after day, this could be either an ordinary heater or some form of night storage heating.

Generally, however, it is simply a question of providing some kind of background heat that will prevent condensation from forming, and probably the most effective way of doing this is to install tubular low-wattage heaters as used in greenhouses. These can be bought in multiples of 305mm (1ft) which are rated at 60 watts each, and two or three of these placed at strategic points around the workshop can make all the difference.

Most of us tend to cut down on woodworking during the winter months as a cold workshop or garage is far from inviting, and this means that machines and tools are left unused for long periods. Before 'putting them to bed' for the winter, clean any sawdust off the machines (if left, it will attract moisture), then spray with a light oil such as WD40; finally, cover with old blankets, tarpaulins or, best of all, the kind of cover sold in garden centres for protecting mowers, strimmers and so on. You can get the best of all worlds by moving all your machines together under one cover to make a kind of tent, and then placing a tubular heater under it as well.

There are several ways to deal with hand tools that are not going to be used for some time. They can be wiped with camellia oil, which is used by the Japanese as it prevents rust but does not mark the wood, or sprayed lightly with

WD40; some woodworkers make up their own concoctions, but in any case before using the tools again you should wipe off any oil that remains.

Another way is to wrap the tools in VPI paper, which is often used by manufacturers to wrap around power tools of various kinds; however, it is not widely available and you may have to undertake quite a search to find it.

Silica gel tablets are particularly useful for protecting small items like nuts, bolts, screws and so on. The tablets are hygroscopic, which means that they attract and absorb moisture from the air; if and when the tablets become damp, they can simply be dried off and reused as necessary.

In all cases, your tools should be kept in a locked cupboard or tool chest.

USING SPACE EFFECTIVELY

When setting up your workshop, you will need to think seriously about your requirements, as these will affect the layout of your workshop radically. For instance, it's no good considering installing comparatively large and heavy fixed machinery such as a bandsaw, radial-arm saw or universal machine in a garden shed measuring perhaps 3.6 x 2.4m (12 x 8ft). Not only do they all take up room, but they also need a lot of working space and a really solid floor. A radial-arm saw, for instance, needs a length of about 3.6m (12ft) so that you can make the most of the variety of jobs it can do; similarly, you will need a lot of working space behind a bandsaw in order to hold the sawn timber as it comes off. Don't forget that you will also need room for the job you are working on, and if this happens to be a large object like a wardrobe it will soon make its presence felt.

3 **A TRADITIONAL WORKBENCH**

Another question of space arises when you have to decide what kind of workbench you want and where to put it. The traditional design shown in **fig 3** is definitely one for a professional woodworker or serious amateur and will take up a considerable amount of room. It does, however, have the advantage of space for storing tools underneath it and in the tray along the back.

As an alternative, why not consider one of the new designs of Workcentre, as shown in **fig 4**? This allows you to mount a portable circular saw, a jigsaw or a router by fixing the tool to a steel sole-plate which is clamped in place so that they are all quickly interchangeable. This type of Workcentre is a very desirable piece of equipment for the majority of woodworkers, who can only work in the evenings or at weekends. The top of the bench usually measures about 600mm (24in) square and the whole thing folds up and can be hung on the wall for real space economy.

Another bench that can be folded and hung up is the much-loved Workmate. This is so well

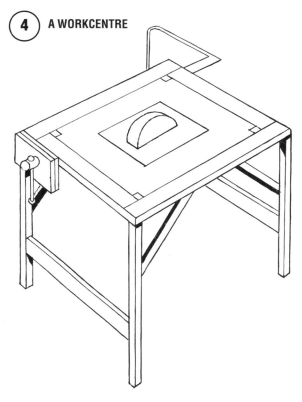

4 A WORKCENTRE

known that it needs no description; it does have the advantage that if any jobs call for heavy hammering (although they are few and far between in most modern woodwork) the Workmate can take it. The scope of both Workcentres and the Workmate is greatly increased if you use them in conjunction with a roller stand (a design is provided on page 97), as it means that you will be able to handle much larger boards.

The most economical and effective use of space can be determined if you make a scale plan of your workshop and then cut out a piece of card to the same scale for each item of your equipment, so that you can lay them on the plan and move them around to achieve the best result.

DUST EXTRACTION

Almost all modern woodwork machines and power tools have some provision for the removal of dust, in the form of either a take-off point for a hose or, in the case of small tools, an integral dust bag which can be taken off and replaced after emptying.

Power tools such as jigsaws, sanders, biscuit jointers and so on have take-off points which can be connected to a domestic vacuum cleaner; these use a comparatively high pressure but a low flow rate. On the other hand, standing machines like bandsaws, thicknessers, radial-arm saws and so on need a high air flow but only low pressure. The two types must therefore not be connected to the same extraction system as their requirements are so different. Another point to bear in mind is that with the kind of workshop dust extractor used for standing machines, the hose diameter is at least 100mm (4in), and in reducing this down to 29mm (1¹⁄₁₆in) for power tools much of the effectiveness is lost.

There is a range of dust extraction kits available, from the smallest which can deal with only one machine at a time and have to be moved around, to the largest design which can cope with three machines at a time. The smallest are about 600 x 355 x 1400mm high (24 x 14 x 55in high) and the largest 1450 x 810 x 2010mm high (57 x 32 x 79in high). There is also a small wall-mounted model which can be installed in an uncluttered corner of the workshop and connected to the machine being used by a hose.

GOGGLES, MASKS, AND RESPIRATORS

Some form of eye protection is essential where there is a likelihood of wood chips flying about – working on the lathe or on a sawbench are two examples. There is a wide range of goggles available and the prices are very reasonable, so there is no excuse for not using them; make sure the design you choose can be worn over normal spectacles.

Woodworking is obviously a very dusty occupation and it is imperative that you wear some form of protection for your nasal passages, throat and lungs. There is a choice between masks, which are designed to fit over just the nose and mouth, and respirators, which fit on to the head like a helmet.

Masks are really only suitable when you are likely to spend no more than half an hour or so working. Although manufacturers try hard to make them comfortable, the fact remains that they soon cause perspiration around the edges, and if you wear spectacles they will almost certainly mist over quickly, making it difficult to see.

For prolonged wear in the workshop in the knowledge that you are fully protected, a respirator is ideal. This is made to fit on the head and in position by adjustable straps, and has a visor which covers the whole of the face and is fitted with comfortable sealing pads which can be worn over a beard. Fresh air enters through filters situated on the top of the head band and is blown gently down over the face by a battery-powered fan, and as this is at a slightly higher pressure no outside air can get in – a great advantage for men with a beard. You then have the benefits of constant fresh air, no misting over of spectacles, and a high degree of protection afforded by the visor. There are two models: one has a four-hour battery and the other an eight-hour one, and a battery charger is supplied in both cases.

USING ELECTRICITY

One of the most common hazards in the workshop is electric cable trailing across the floor, waiting to trip you up.

In some cases – for example on sawbenches, sanders, bandsaws and lathes – it may be possible to fix cup-hooks into the ceiling and lead the cable through them, so that it arrives at the machine from above and causes as little inconvenience as possible. You could also fix a counterweight, such as a small plastic bag of sand, somewhere in the loop of the cable so that it will pull it up to the ceiling when the cable is not in use.

RCD ADAPTOR (RESIDUAL CURRENT DEVICE)

This device cuts off the electrical current immediately if there is any change in voltage due to an accident or a power surge, and is particularly recommended when you are working out of doors, where cables can be cut accidentally or water can get into the circuit. It is important that the device is plugged into the mains socket itself and not merely wired into the circuit somewhere else.

NVR (NO-VOLT RELEASE) SWITCHES

These switches are fitted as standard to all industrial-rated machines and are strongly recommended for fitting to lathes, bandsaws, circular saws, spindle moulders, sanders and similar machinery.

The best way to explain how they work is to imagine a scenario where you are happily sawing away on your sawbench and suddenly everything stops because there is a power cut. While waiting for the power to be restored you go into the house for a cup of tea, and during this time the power comes back on. When you return to the workshop you have to remember that the saw will be working again and it is in the failure to appreciate this that the danger lies and accidents happen.

An NVR switch will prevent an electric motor from re-starting after an accidental cut-off; the motor can only be turned on again by using the on-off switch. The device should be fitted by a professional electrician because motor size and phasing have to be considered.

FIRE HAZARDS

It is perhaps not as widely known as it should be that heaps of fine sawdust can be self-combustible and are, therefore, potential fire raisers. Many fires in woodworking factories occur an hour or two after the factory has closed and are caused by the residual heat in the machine igniting any heaps of sawdust situated around it. Bear in mind also that the dust has been gently heating up all day.

This is one of the reasons why the Health and Safety Executive recommends that dust extractors are located outside the workshop (generally impractical in our case) or in a corner, where any dust igniting into sparks can burn out without causing further damage. Obviously the risk can be greatly reduced if most of the dust can be extracted after every session of work.

One further point: heaps of damp rags, including all those used for applying white spirit, polish or varnishes are also capable of self-combustion and should be disposed of immediately after use.

FIRST AID

Accidents in the workshop tend to be dramatic, with gory gashes to hands and fingers at the top of the list. Something more than the usual collection of plain adhesive tapes and cotton wool is called for, and it is worth purchasing an industrial-type first aid kit which contains proper wound dressings.

Chapter 2

TIMBERS AND BOARDS

Choosing, measuring and buying timber is an area of woodworking that is fraught with problems for beginners and even, at times, the experts. There are many factors involved such as seasoning, strength, ease of working and polishing and the possibility of defects, and the whole procedure can become a massive headache. The information that follows should enable you to all avoid the more common pitfalls.

CLASSIFICATION

Timber is divided into two classes: hardwoods and softwoods. Hardwoods come from deciduous, broadleaved trees which shed their leaves in winter in temperate climates. More scientifically, hardwoods have open cells (as distinct from self-contained cells) which carry moisture throughout the tree; the cells are therefore moisture-conducting rather than moisture-absorbing. The term 'hard' does not relate to the actual hardness of the wood – thus, obeche is softer than most softwoods, but is nevertheless classed as a hardwood.

Softwoods come from coniferous (cone-bearing) trees with needle-pointed leaves. They are non-porous in that the cells are not open-ended as in hardwoods, and the sap passes from cell to cell through fragile party walls.

CONVERSION METHODS

The way in which the log (the tree trunk with all branches cut off and the ends sawn square) is converted is determined by the need to obtain as much usable timber as possible and, in the case of hardwoods, the requirement that the sawn planks or 'boards' should exhibit a specified kind of grain pattern.

Dealing first with softwoods, **fig 1** overleaf illustrates the main types of machined timbers and mouldings into which they are converted and the patterns you will find displayed at the timber merchant.

Hardwood conversion is more complicated. **Fig 2** shows how a log would be converted if the grain pattern is immaterial, as in the case of beech, which is suitable only for rails, legs etc., and not for use in large widths. The plank shown is 75mm (3in) thick, and **fig A** shows it cut into five 12mm (½in) boards; **fig B** cut down the centre to form two pieces; **fig C** cut into four 16mm (⅝in) or (not shown) three 22mm (⅞in) boards; **fig D** cut into two halves; and **fig E** cut into thick quartering.

Some other ways to convert hardwood are also shown, where **fig F** is 'through-and-through' sawn, also called 'slash sawn'; **fig G** billet-sawn; **fig H** plain sawn; **fig I** modern quarter-sawn; and **fig J** true quarter-sawn. The way in which the log is cut has a marked effect on the grain pattern of the resulting boards, depending on whether the cut is tangential or radial. This point is further developed in **fig 3**, where the tangential cut **a** yields no figure; **b**, which is half tangential and half radial, reveals a small amount of figure; while **c** and **d** are both parallel with the medullary rays and are therefore both radial cuts which give the full figure.

1 SOFTWOOD CONVERSION: MACHINED TIMBERS, MOULDINGS AND PATTERNS

SQUARE-EDGED

SPLAYED

BEVELLED

CHAMFERED

ARRIS   ROUNDED   NOSING

VEE-GROOVE   HOLLOW   SQUARE GROOVE

THROATING   REBATED

BEADED   OVOLO-BEADED

TONGUED, GROOVED AND BEADED

TONGUE AND VEE-GROOVE

PLAIN TONGUE AND GROOVE

TONGUED AND REBATED

FEATHER-EDGED

VARIOUS MOULDING PROFILES

3

HARDWOOD CONVERSION: THE EFFECT ON GRAIN PATTERN OF TANGENTIAL AND RADIAL CUTS

a

b

c

d

2 HARDWOOD CONVERSION: PLANKS AND LOGS

A

B

C

D

E

F   G   H   I   J

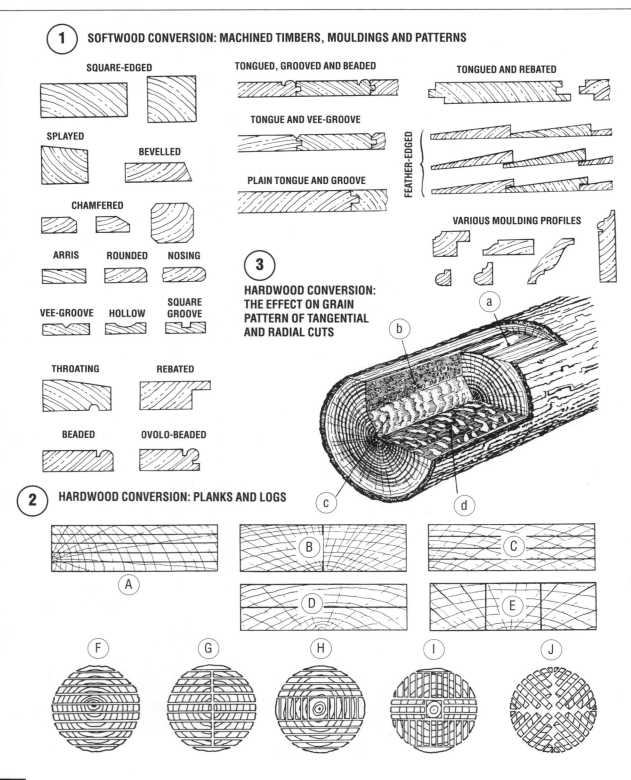

HEART AND HEARTWOOD

Any reference to 'heart' as opposed to 'heartwood' really refers to 'pith'. On the end grain of a complete section of round wood there is a tiny pith, which is actually the compressed original sapling around which all subsequent growth was formed.

Various hazards and environmental circumstances during the growth of a tree, such as its need to resist gales and storms or cope with unsuitable soil or site conditions, will cause it to develop growth characteristics as it reacts to these stresses. A typical example is where the pith on the end of a felled log is offset from the centre, which is an indicator of extreme stress: the same feature is frequently found in the cross-section of a branch, where the growth has become distorted because of the strength required to hold the branch up against the force of gravity.

In the conversion of logs to timber (here we are talking generally of the main stem or trunk), the first cut is often made through the pith. It is called a 'breaking cut' and is made to relieve much of the growth stress; this is why splitting logs down their length into half rounds is recommended.

When relatively small trees like pine, spruce and similar softwoods are converted, the use of the breaking cut often means that some boards contain the pith. You would be wise to reject these, because a relatively small volume of wood is involved in which the stresses are closely confined. Smaller-diameter branches and the 'lops and tops' which are trimmed off before felling will also have a pith, but they should be safe to use for woodworking if they are dried carefully.

DEFECTS IN TIMBER

With timber the price it is, you need to know what defects you are likely to find. These are illustrated in **fig 4**.

Avoid timber containing knots as shown in **fig A**, except in softwoods where firm, tight knots up to 19mm (¾in) diameter are permissible; however, cut out dead knots which have a black ring around them.

Fig B shows a 'waney' edge consisting of bark and sapwood which is sometimes left on hardwoods, mainly on the outer planks; both must be removed.

Fig C illustrates felling or compression 'shakes' (splits which do not necessarily penetrate right through the wood) and the parts containing them will have to be cut out. They

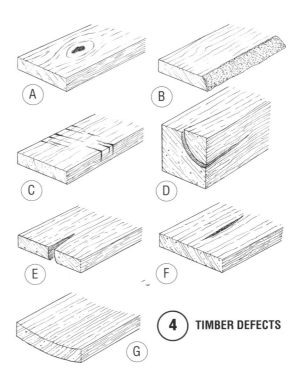

4 TIMBER DEFECTS

are caused by the stresses involved in felling the tree.

Fig D shows a 'cup' shake caused by the heartwood drying out more quickly than the rest, and the timber should be discarded unless you can saw away the worst affected areas.

The 'end' shake in **fig E** should also be cut away, although you can saw the timber lengthwise into strips if your requirements allow it.

Fig F illustrates a shake which can either extend partway through the board or penetrate it completely; in both cases, the affected area must be cut away. Sometimes this defect does not become apparent until you are actually working on the plank.

Fig G shows a warped board. If the warping is crosswise, as shown, the board will have to be cut into narrow strips lengthwise; conversely, if the warping is lengthwise, the board can be sawn into short lengths across it.

BLOCKBOARDS, CHIPBOARDS AND MULTI-PLYWOOD

These boards, shown in **fig 5**, have now been largely superseded by medium density fibreboards (MDF), also shown, which respond to machining with accurate, crisp edges; all the other boards require some kind of edge treatment such as an attached moulding to cover the comparatively rough finish.

Blockboard consists of a core of softwood strips glued together side by side and contained between two face veneers (it is then called 'three ply') or two face veneers each side (five ply). It is strong enough for general cabinet work and it can also be used as a groundwork for veneering.

Chipboard is a softwood-chip-plus-adhesive mixture which is pressed between heated platens (rollers) until it is the correct thickness. There are high, medium and low grades of

(5) MAN-MADE BOARDS

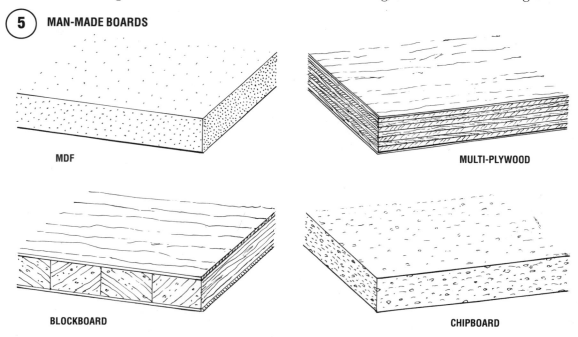

MDF

MULTI-PLYWOOD

BLOCKBOARD

CHIPBOARD

density for different jobs, but in fact even the highest density does not give a board suitable for anything more than non-loadbearing and light constructional uses.

MDF has largely taken over from multi-plywood in furniture construction as it is considerably cheaper and more widely available. An additional problem in purchasing multi-plywood lies in selecting the correct grade, as there are so many to choose from; nevertheless, it is still widely used in industry, where specific characteristics such as resistance to mould, fungus or water are essential.

MDF (MEDIUM DENSITY FIBRE-BOARD)

This is a comparatively new man-made board which has largely superseded chipboard and plywood in furniture-making and woodworking as it has several advantages. These include being uniform in its composition and completely stable, so that it will not warp or twist; these characteristics allow manufacturers to employ it in computer-controlled furniture-making, caravan construction and similar productions. Without going too deeply into the technicalities of its manufacture, MDF is made by reducing natural wood into a fibrous mass, which is impregnated with a formaldehyde-based resin adhesive and then formed into mats that are subjected to heat and pressure to produce the boards.

The standard size of a board is 2440 x 1220mm (8 x 4ft) and the thicknesses vary between 2.5mm and 50mm (⅛in and 2in); the thicknesses generally available from DIY stores and builders' merchants are 6mm, 10mm, 12mm and 19mm (¼in, ⅜in, ½in and ¾in). The colour is a nondescript pale brown with no grain pattern, perfectly smooth faces and edges that need no sanding. It is ideal as a base for veneering provided the adhesive is not diluted with water, and the standard white PVA woodworking adhesive can be used for both veneering and general work. MDF can also be painted with good results.

Working MDF with routers, saws (both hand and power), jigsaws, bandsaws and the like calls for the use of TCT (tungsten-carbide-tipped) tools, as the rock-hard adhesive will quickly blunt anything else. The edges are particularly susceptible to bruising if the boards are not handled and stacked carefully; nevertheless, they can be planed or routed easily, although if you are applying a moulded edge with a router you should avoid any acute angles or sharp profiles as they can be chipped or bruised quite easily.

Fastening MDF with screws, nails or staples is straightforward provided you observe a few guidelines. Firstly, if possible use the type of screw designed for chipboards and MDF boards called 'Gold screws', which are widely used in Europe but are not so well known in Britain except from specialist suppliers. They have a honey-coloured wax coating (hence the name) to make them easier to insert. The screws are threaded along their whole length and can be driven into the face of the board without drilling a pilot hole as the thread bites into the fibres instead of pushing them apart. If you are putting a screw into an edge, however, a pilot hole is advisable and should be at least three-quarters the diameter of the screw. When driving screws into the face, make sure that they are at least 25mm (1in) away from any corner and about 150mm (6in) apart.

Dowels can be used, but they must be a comparatively loose fit into their holes so that they do not burst the fibres apart. The usual recommendation is that the holes should be 0.1mm (about ¹⁄₆₄in) larger than the dowel; this could be implemented by wrapping a paper collar around the dowel and drilling the hole to fit. Router cutters should be treated in the same manner.

MDF has three main disadvantages. The boards are heavy, and one board is just about as much as one man can manage to carry – a home-made carrier as shown in **fig 6** can help. Even better, many suppliers will cut the boards for you on their premises and will do this to very accurate dimensions, although you may have to pay a little extra.

Water is the enemy of ordinary-grade MDF, and even heavy condensation will cause the surface to blister. A water-resistant board is available from some suppliers but you may have to seek it out.

The worst disadvantage is the dust created when working. This is a hazard with all man-made boards, but the dust from MDF is very fine and penetrating and you must wear a good design of mask or respirator so that you do not inhale it.

NOMINAL AND FINISHED SIZES

It is important to understand the difference between these two terms, as it can affect the price of timber dramatically. Nominal sizes are those to which the timber is cut at the sawmill, while finished (or machined) sizes are those which result after the timber has been re-sawn and planed.

Take as an example a piece which measures, say, 305mm (12in) wide by 25mm (1in) thick in nominal size; this will be reduced to about 300 x 22mm (11¹³⁄₁₆ x ⅞in bare) as finished size, but will still be referred to as 305 x 25mm (12 x 1in) nominal. At this stage, length does not enter into the matter. It follows, then, that if you present a cutting list to a timber supplier which calls for 25mm (1in) finished thickness, he will have to prepare it from 29mm or 32mm (1⅛in or 1¼in) stock, which means wasted timber for which you will have to pay.

Softwood is charged at so much 'per metre run', the price varying according to the pattern of its cross-section. The more complicated the cross-section of a piece of moulding, the more expensive it will be. A plain 50 x 25mm (2 x 1in) batten will be cheaper, and roughly half the cost of one 100 x 50mm (4 x 2in), which has double the content.

Hardwoods are measured according to the

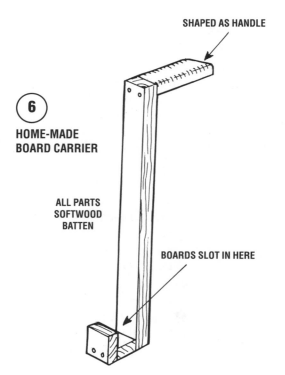

SHAPED AS HANDLE

6

HOME-MADE BOARD CARRIER

ALL PARTS
SOFTWOOD
BATTEN

BOARDS SLOT IN HERE

cubic content and many hardwood suppliers still use the imperial measurements of inches, feet and cubic feet, as using metric measures can result in astronomical figures and decimal points can easily go astray. The vital point to remember when calculating cubic content is that all the dimensions must be expressed in the same units; thus, they should all be either metric or imperial.

As an example, consider a plank 12ft long by 12in wide by 1in thick. The first step is to convert the 12ft into inches by multiplying by 12, which gives 144in; the calculation is then (144 x 12 x 1) divided by 1728 (the number of cubic inches in a cubic foot) – the answer is obviously 1cu ft.

Things can become complicated in real life when the dimensions are difficult to convert into inches. As an example, consider a plank 10ft 7in long by 13½in wide by 1in thick. It is possible to calculate the cubic content by using the method given above but it would be quite laborious, so in the wood trade both time and trouble are saved by using sets of tables contained in a small book called the *Hoppus Measure*. Anyone likely to become involved in measuring timber is advised to buy one.

MOISTURE CONTENT FOR DOMESTIC WOODWORK

Moisture content can range between 8 per cent for woodwork near to heat sources such as shelves over radiators, mantelpieces, fireplace surrounds and flooring laid over hot water pipes, to 15 per cent for general joinery such as doors, window frames and roof timbers.

Ordinary domestic furniture, panelling and musical instruments such as pianos need about 12 per cent moisture content where there is more or less continuous central heating, while bedroom furniture in rooms where the heating is intermittent needs 13–14 per cent.

MEASURING MOISTURE CONTENT

Moisture content is normally established by using a moisture meter. This measures the amount of electrical current flowing between its two probes, which are pushed into the wood being tested.

For those who do not have such a meter, it is possible to use the old-fashioned method of comparing the wet weight (also known as the initial weight) and the dry (final) weight of a wood sample. The initial weight of the sample should be about 0.22kg (½lb), and the size will depend upon the density of the wood being tested. If it is taken from a plank that is being seasoned in the open it should come from the middle part, as the ends of the planks will usually be drier.

The sample must be weighed as accurately as possible and a set of good-quality kitchen scales should do this well enough. Note down the initial weight. The sample now needs to be dried: place it in an electric or gas oven with the temperature set at 100°C (212° F) and leave for half an hour or so. Look at it every few minutes to check that it is not scorching and remove it immediately if it is. After half an hour, take the sample out of the oven and weigh it; then replace in the oven for about ten minutes before removing it finally and weighing again. If these two weights are equal, it can safely be assumed that all moisture has been driven out, and the sample now has its dry (final) weight.

To calculate the moisture content, multiply the weight of moisture lost (that is, the difference between the initial and final weights) by 100 and divide the result by the dry weight, to give the percentage moisture content. As an example (worked in metric weights): if the initial weight is 227g and the final weight 170g, then 227 minus 170 equals 57g; 57 multiplied by 100 equals 5700 which, divided by 170, gives a moisture content of 33 per cent (rounded off).

TIMBER GRADES

Apart from log-sawn material – that is, timber which has waney edges or one square edge – timber is always graded according to the visual quality of one face. The following are the best-known grades:

FAS (Firsts and Seconds) refers to boards with one face free from all defects. The reverse face may contain certain minor defects specified by the grading rules of the exporting country.
No 1 C & S (No 1 Common and Selects) are the next grade down, and again one face will be clean enough, its precise condition varying with the shipper and the tree species. There may be one or two comparatively small departures from FAS standards, such as a higher proportion of sapwood or slight but sound discoloration, and more blemishes will be permitted on the reverse.
Merchantable ('Select Merchantable' and 'Standard and Better') are other lower grades; the last, usually, refers to South-East Asian woods of fairly plain appearance, while the first is not encountered very often.
Home-grown hardwoods are the timbers with the greatest interest for home woodworkers and are usually graded as first quality (or prime) or second quality, with merchantable sometimes being available as well.

Any given parcel of timber is a mixture of boards from many trees, and not necessarily all from their boles – some will come from limbs and branches. The important point, however, is that although higher grades of timber are assessed fresh from the saw, to give the maximum freedom from defects and the minimum variation in grain and texture, beauty is still in the eye of the beholder. Plenty of interesting material can be selected from even the lowest grades.

TERMS USED FOR DIMENSIONED TIMBER

Once a log has been converted (that is, sawn) the following terms are used to describe the sawn pieces, depending on size.

Batten (softwood) 127–203mm (5–8in) wide by 50–102mm (2–4in) thick. A common size is 50 x 19mm (2 x ¾in).
Baulk A log squared up ready for further conversion. Minimum size 115mm (4½in) square, but usually much larger.
Board (hardwood) Any width up to 32mm (1¼in) thick.

Deal (softwood) 230–280mm (9–11in) wide by 50–102mm (2–4in) thick.

Flitch (hardwood) Minimum size 204 x 102mm (8 x 4in).

Flitch (softwood) Minimum size 305 x 102mm (12 x 4in).

Plank 280mm (11in) or more wide by 50–150mm (2–6in) thick.

Scantling 50–115mm (2–4½in) wide by 50–102mm (2–4in) thick.

Slab Random pieces sawn from the outside of the log to square it up. Convex on one side and flat on the other, and the bark is often left on. Regarded as waste, but useful for covering stacked timber.

Strip Under 102 x 50mm (4 x 2in).

Planks and boards are sold either 'square-edged' (S/E), when the edges have been sawn at right angles to the face, or 'waney-edged' (W/E), when the natural edge of the tree is left on one or both edges.

Chapter 3

JIGS, ACCESSORIES AND TECHNIQUES FOR MACHINE WORK

Before we look at a range of jigs, aids and devices for use in machine work, here is a survey of the latest woodworking machines and their specifications. Note that in January 1995, an EC standard for both power tools and machinery came into effect and products which comply with it bear a CB mark. If you are buying a new machine, do check that it carries the mark or ask the supplier if it complies with the standard.

BANDSAW

To many woodworkers, this is the machine around which they will build the rest of their workshop and it is certainly one of the most versatile and the safest.

Basically, a bandsaw consists of a continuous saw blade which is driven around two wheels mounted one above the other; the lower one does the actual driving, while the top one is an idler and is carried around by the saw blade. You can obtain three-wheeled bandsaws, but they are restricted to smaller woodwork as the maximum depth you can saw is 76mm (3in) and the blade is put under more stress by having to travel around the extra wheel. There is a choice of single-speed, two-speed and also variable-speed machines; if you want to saw metals and plastics as well as wood you will need a two-speed or a variable-speed model, as the single speed is too high for the job. Some models are supplied without stands and can be mounted on benches and stored after use; even those which come fixed to a stand can be separated from it, although you then have a redundant stand. This feature is essential if you have to work in a confined space with no room for a permanently fixed machine.

Two important factors to consider are the cutting depth and the throat depth. The first is self-explanatory and varies from 152mm (6in) up to 205mm (8$\frac{1}{16}$in); most woodworkers find that the first-mentioned depth is more than adequate and it is only those who have to saw out heavy blanks for bowl turning who need the greater depth.

Throat depth refers to the distance between the saw blade and the casing of the body which will allow timber to be passed through freely, and varies from 267mm (10$\frac{1}{2}$in) to 343mm (13$\frac{1}{2}$in). Most machines are around the 308mm (12$\frac{1}{16}$in) depth, and as 305mm (12in – the imperial foot) is still one of the dimensions met with most often, it is probably the best choice.

The tables also vary in size and you should buy the largest you can afford as it will give you more control over the work. All tables can tilt and have some form of control gear so that you can clamp the table at the desired angle, and most manufacturers include such accessories as a right-angle fence for straightforward ripsawing plus a mitre fence and a circle guide.

All machines have opening doors for access to the wheels when changing blades, and some have a built-in safety feature which prevents you from switching on the motor while the doors are open. You will also need to open them for 'tracking' the saw blade, which means making sure that it is positioned centrally on the width of the wheels, otherwise the rubber tyre will wear unevenly and at worst the blade could come off. To adjust it, you will need to tilt the upper idling wheel by a fraction, and there is a hand wheel at the back for doing this while turning the blade by hand.

There are two more adjustments to be made, namely tensioning the blade and adjusting the two guides. The first is necessary after fitting a new blade and is effected by raising or lowering the upper wheel by means of a hand wheel at the top of the casing, in accordance with an indicator scale for different widths of blade. If the indicator scale is missing, the length of saw required can be found by raising the upper wheel to its fullest extent and then lowering it by 20mm (¾in) and running a length of string around both wheels. When adjusting the guides, you will find that one is located just below the table and the other just above the timber being sawn.

USING YOUR BANDSAW

The following tips should help you get the best results from your bandsaw.

Make sure you have a selection of blades available instead of trying to make one do everything. You will need wide blades for straight cuts and narrow ones for curves, remembering that there should be a minimum of two teeth actually in contact with the workpiece. Fine blades on thick work will tend to burn, as the gullets on the teeth will be unable to clear the waste quickly enough.

Always keep the guide to a point just above the workpiece: this not only makes the blade run more truly but also supports it where the strain is greatest.

Fine teeth are used for thin, hard materials and coarse teeth for softer, thicker ones. With fine teeth, the best results are achieved with a high saw speed and a slow rate of feed – with coarse teeth, a high saw speed and a faster feed rate.

Fig 1 oppposite illustrates the profiles of regular and skip teeth. The latter have a shallower cutting angle and therefore a larger gullet

TOOTH FORMAT: BLADE SELECTION

Width	Skip tooth	Regular tooth
Length up to 1778mm (70in)		
6mm (¼in)	6	10 – 14 – 24
10mm (⅜in)	4 – 6	10 – 14
13mm (½in)	3 – 4 – 6	14
Length from 1778mm to 2234mm (70in to 88in)		
3mm (⅛in)		14
5mm (³⁄₁₆in)		10 – 14
6mm (¼in)	4 – 6	10 – 14 – 24
10mm (⅜in)	3 – 4 – 6	10 – 14
13mm (½in)	3 – 4 – 6	10 – 14 – 24
Length over 2234mm (88in)		
3mm (⅛in)		14
5mm (³⁄₁₆in)		10 – 14
6mm (¼in)	4 – 6	10 – 14 – 24
10mm (⅜in)	3 – 4 – 6	10 – 14
13mm (½in)	3 – 4 – 6	10 – 14 – 24
16mm (⅝in)	3 – 4 – 6	
19mm (¾in)	3 – 4 –	10

RADIUS CUTTING

Blade width	Minimum radius
3mm (⅛in)	10mm (⅜in)
5mm (³⁄₁₆in)	13mm (½in)
6mm (¼in)	19mm (¾in)
10mm (⅜in)	28mm (1¹⁄₁₆in)
13mm (½in)	64mm (2½in)

The information in these tables is reproduced by kind permission of the Axminster Power Tool Centre (see Suppliers).

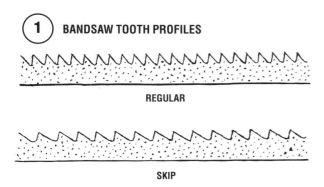

1 BANDSAW TOOTH PROFILES

REGULAR

SKIP

which clears waste away quickly: for general work use a blade with six skip teeth per 25mm (1in), and for deep cuts over 50mm (2in) a three- or four-skip blade. The tables opposite show the tooth format of different blade widths and the minimum radii of curves that can be cut with them.

SAWBENCH

The parts of a typical sawbench are as follows:

Table This should be as large as possible; generally, its size depends on the price you pay.

Tilting arbor A mechanical device, usually operated by a hand wheel, which allows the saw blade to be tilted at an angle. This is preferable to the alternative design of sawbench, in which the table tilts instead of the saw blade, as it is safer.

Channels or grooves in the table surface These act as guides when using proprietary or home-made jigs.

Blade It is recommended that you do not fit a blade which is smaller than ⁹⁄₁₀ths of the largest blade the sawbench will accept, as stated in the manufacturer's specification. TCT (tungsten-carbide-tipped) blades cut best and last longest, although they have a wider kerf

(3.2mm) than the alternative carbon-alloy steel blades. HSS (high-speed steel) blades are better not used at the speeds encountered on sawbenches as it is possible that they could shatter. A 250mm (10in) diameter, 40-tooth, general-purpose blade, plus a 28-tooth blade for coarse work, make a good combination to start with. Other kinds include thin kerf ripsaw blades, where the kerf width varies from 2mm to 3mm according to the diameter, plus fine crosscut, extra fine and heavy duty ripsaw blades.

Crown guard On some types of machine this is attached to the riving knife (see below), but in any case it should never be more than 13mm (½in) above the blade, or the same distance behind it. The crown guard is the chief means of protecting your hands and if it has to be removed to allow a special accessory or jig to be used, then feather boards or guard boards must be used.

Riving knife This keeps the parts of the sawn wood apart and prevents any binding and kickback which may occur.

Rip fence This is the fence against which the wood is held when ripsawing it, and is adjustable to a range of widths. Most woodworkers like to fasten a strip of hardwood to it to make it deeper and longer, so that it can be fixed at both ends of the table to ensure it is precisely parallel to the saw blade.

Dust extraction This facility is fitted to all modern machines.

Motor The power of this depends on the diameter of the saw blade and typical ratings are:

200mm (8in)	⅓hp
250mm (10in)	1½hp
305mm (12in)	3hp
400mm (15¾in)	4½hp

JIGSAW

After a bandsaw and a sawbench, a jigsaw is probably the most useful power tool you can have. It makes easy work of what used to be the drudgery of sawing curves on the outside of a panel, or cutting circles and shapes in the centre, using a coping saw or padsaw. As a bonus, you can easily fit blades to cut metals, plastics or even ceramic tiles.

The blade is clamped into the machine with one or two screws or, on one or two models, with a spring-loaded lever. It is essential to remember that the saw blade cuts only on the upward movement of the up-and-down stroke, which means that the face side of your work must always be on the bottom as the sawing action can break out the top surface and this can be disastrous on a plastic-faced board.

Most models have a 'pendulum' action which causes the blade to swing backwards and forwards while cutting and this feels odd until you get used to it, but it certainly means that you can saw straight cuts more quickly and easily; however, it is awkward to use on curved cuts. There is, of course, a switch which allows the amount of pendulum action to be regulated.

Another feature on many models is that the sole-plate can be adjusted to give a 45-degree cut on either side and there is usually a calibrated scale enabling you to do this, but it pays to check with a mitre square.

Variable speed control is fitted to all except the least expensive machines and speeds are quoted in strokes per minute, up to 3200.

As you would expect, the blade is the most important part of the machine. When you buy replacement blades, take care to check that they will fit your model as they are not very often interchangeable. Generally blades will cut

between 50mm (2in) and 65mm (2½in) softwood – but be guided by the manufacturer's recommendations.

One model, made by Black and Decker, has an intriguing feature in its 'scroll saw action'. This allows the blade itself to be turned to any angle relative to the body, enabling very small circles to be cut – and if you want novelty, you can still cut while pushing the machine sideways!

All jigsaws have some provision for dust extraction, and it is worthwhile taking full advantage of this as the upward motion of the saw blade throws up quantities of dust – particularly from man-made boards – which is not only harmful to your lungs but also obscures the guideline.

PORTABLE CIRCULAR SAW

If your work involves cutting up large pieces of man-made boards, then you need one of these. Sawing a 2240 x 1220mm (8 x 4ft) sheet of hardboard is awkward enough, but to cut a piece of the same size of 25mm (1in) MDF using any other tool would be hazardous to say the least, and could not be done safely even on a bandsaw or sawbench. You could use a jigsaw, but it would be slow and difficult to cut in a straight line even if the saw were guided by a straightedge.

Some woodworkers hold such a sheet down on to trestles or roller stands, but although better, this is not really satisfactory unless you have a helper to hold the offcut, which would otherwise crash to the floor. A good plan is to lay the sheet on some blocks or thick timber placed on the floor so that it stands about 100mm (4in) above it, and then cut the sheet by kneeling or crouching down to operate the portable saw; as the maximum depth it will cut is 70mm (2¾in), this allows plenty of clearance.

A very important point to consider is the weight: the heaviest saws weigh about 7kg (16lb) and the lightest about 4kg (9½lb). If you only use the saw occasionally, one of the lighter models will do everything you need.

Speeds vary from 4500 to 5500rpm regardless of the weight: some of the heavier saws need strong handling when they are switched on, and the starting torque can be rather disconcerting. All the saws are single speed except one, the Festo, which has variable speed control and a soft-start, and is correspondingly expensive.

All the saws are supplied with TCT (tungsten-carbide-tipped) blades; although the general rule that 'the more teeth, the better the finish' applies, it is not significant as all the blades give an adequate finish. Cutting depths vary from 62mm (2⁷⁄₁₆in) to 70mm (2¾in).

The way the machine handles, both in and out of use, is important. All are fitted with a blade guard, which rides over the work while sawing is in progress and falls down to cover the blade afterwards; other accessories include an adjustable fence for ripsawing, a facility for tilting the blade at an angle and (usually) a lock-off button for the power. Make sure that all these work smoothly and easily, as you often have to adjust them with one hand while holding the machine with the other.

Most saw blades can be changed by using a spanner in conjunction with a spindle lock and this feature is well worth having, as on one or two machines either the blade has to be jammed into a block of spare wood or a screwdriver has to be inserted through a hole in the blade to prevent it moving. All the machines are noisy and all create quantities of dust, which should be ejected either through a spout that directs it away from the user, or through a nozzle into a collection bag via an exhaust hose.

POWER PLANE

Power planes are, of course, the powered versions of the familiar hand planes. A typical example has a motor which drives a cutter block by means of a rubber belt at speeds varying from 12000rpm to 19000rpm, although this is not a guide to the depth of cut which depends on the wattage.

The cutter block has two blades clamped into it; in most cases, these are TCT (tungsten-carbide-tipped) to deal with the abrasive nature of man-made boards, and are thrown away when blunt and a new pair fitted; however, as they are double-sided this takes quite a time. One or two models have HSS (high-speed steel) blades which soon become blunt when used for planing man-made boards, but it is possible to re-sharpen them yourself.

Normally the cutter blades are 82mm (3¼in) wide, compared with the widest cutting iron for a hand plane which is 60mm (2⅜in). While a power plane is ideal for narrow work, it is difficult to plane a large area flat with it because each pass tends to create ridges. This can be overcome by using the power plane first, followed by a hand smoothing plane to remove the ridges, which should result in an accurate and smooth surface.

Less expensive planes remove only 1–1.5mm as a maximum; although this seems small compared with the 2.5mm and 3.6mm depths of cut of the bigger machines, it still represents many passes of a hand plane and should not be dismissed out of hand.

You can rebate with the more expensive models, but the rebate fences and stops are usually extras and have to be purchased separately. Similarly, although most machines have a chip and dust collecting facility, any hosing and collection bags are extras. There should be some kind of spring-loaded guard plate over the end of the cutter block to protect those who habitually curl their fingers around the edge of a hand plane to act as a fence and tend to do the same thing (but only once!) with an unguarded power plane. A useful accessory is the subframe, or inversion stand, which is a kind of cradle that allows you to position the plane upside-down safely so that it can be used as an overhand plane.

Adjustment of the depth of cut is controlled by turning a calibrated knob on the front end of the machine. One manufacturer (Bosch) has gone a step further and can supply a thicknessing attachment to which the plane is fitted, enabling timber to be thicknessed up to 70mm (2¾in) thick by 80mm (3⅛in)wide.

ORBITAL AND RANDOM ORBIT SANDERS

The orbital sander was introduced first, the random orbit machine is comparatively recent. They are the most commonly used portable sanding machines.

The orbital type comes in two sizes – the one-third sheet and the half sheet – the pad sizes being approximately 90 x 184mm (3½ x 7¼in) and 115 x 200mm (4½in by 8in) respectively. The sheet referred to is the standard abrasive one; alternatively, you can buy rolls of abrasive paper either 90mm (3½in) or 115mm (4½in) wide and cut them to length.

The orbital sander has an electric motor

mounted vertically that drives an off-centre shaft, which also rotates eccentrically in an orbit (hence the name); with fine abrasive paper, the tiny circular swirls that are produced are practically unnoticeable, but with coarser grades you may have to glasspaper by hand so as to eliminate them. The platen (or base plate) is mounted flexibly to absorb small imperfections in the surface, and the abrasive paper is held by either sprung clamps or wire clips. If your sander has holes in its pad to enable a fan beneath the motor to suck up the dust, the abrasive paper itself has to be perforated with matching holes in order for it to escape, and this is the case with most machines. Some manufacturers supply a pattern for perforating the holes in the sheet, but if not you will have to make your own.

By their very nature, these machines create a lot of dust and all are fitted with some form of nozzle for dust extraction, so be sure to take full advantage of it and be careful to wear a mask or respirator as well.

The random orbit sander combines the circular motion of a disc sander with a random eccentric pattern. The action is such that it can be used for hard work such as paint removal as well as for fine finishing. An added and very useful bonus is that you can sand across the grain without leaving scratches – something the orbital sander cannot do. Most machines have variable speed control (although the Black and Decker model has only two) and this allows you to cope with heavy stock removal on rough timber or old paintwork, as well as the lightest of touches for finishing.

The designs are all different in the way that the motors are mounted and in the location of the handles, and it is a matter of trying a selection of machines and choosing the one that suits you. All have provision for dust extraction with a paper or canvas bag ready fitted.

The pads that actually do the sanding are backed with Velcro, which makes removal easy. Replacement pads are sold in sets of five or six with a range of grit sizes and at the moment are not widely available: this means that you should check their availability when you buy your machine and try to keep a reasonable stock. Each rubber backing pad has a pattern of extraction holes which must line up with those on the discs themselves to allow the dust to be sucked away, in a similar way to those on the orbital machine.

BISCUIT JOINTERS (HAND JOINTERS)

These machines are comparatively new to British woodworkers but are rapidly gaining in popularity as the 'biscuit joint' is a fast, easily made and effective alternative to mortise and tenoned, dowelled, tongued and some kinds of dovetailed joints.

A typical jointer consists basically of a small-diameter saw which is mounted horizontally in the body of the machine and, in use, protrudes to make an arc-shaped sawcut in the workpiece. A suitable size of biscuit (see **fig 2**) is glued into the sawcut and is shaped so that the unglued half which protrudes can be glued

into a sawcut on the piece to be joined.

As alternatives to the machines which have a fixed motor, you can now buy vertical-motor and tilt-motor models. If you only want to make biscuit joints the horizontal motor will suffice, but with the vertical and tilt motors you will also be able to cut grooves and rebates, and trim panels; in addition, the tilt motor will also make mitred joints.

The biscuits are made of compressed dry beech and swell up when glued into the saw-cuts with a PVA water-based adhesive; this makes joints which are claimed to be superior to traditional ones. The biscuits need to be kept bone dry in an airtight container in the airing cupboard and should never be left exposed to a damp atmosphere for long. If they do show signs of having absorbed moisture, they should be dried off in a microwave oven for a few seconds. The No 0 biscuit is for use with timber or man-made boards up to 12mm (½in) thick, No 10 is for materials up to 18mm (1¹¹⁄₁₆in) thick, and No 20 for materials 19mm (¾in) thick.

The saw blade will eventually wear out and need renewing, and it is worth checking how this is done before you make your choice as on some machines it can be an awkward job.

POWER DRILL

Power drills have come a very long way from the single-speed, no-hammer action models of the old days, and are now available as either mains-powered or cordless (battery-powered).

Most mains-powered models have two speeds as a minimum, a hammer action (also called 'impact' action) for drilling holes in masonry, a reverse gear and a screwdriving and withdrawing facility. The more expensive ones

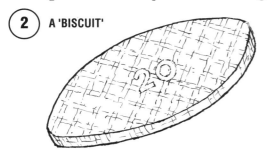

2 A 'BISCUIT'

have speed and torque control, which means that the speed and power can be pre-set when driving screws so that a large number can be driven in with exactly the same power. This avoids the problem that is all too common with other drills, when screws are driven in too far before you can stop the drill.

Smaller models have only a 10mm (⅜in) chuck capacity which is rather restricting, but larger ones will accept 13mm (½in) drills. Many now have keyless chucks, which is a great advantage as there is no key to be lost and the drills are held more securely.

The depths that can be drilled in various materials depend on the wattage, and the following are typical examples:

Wattage	Wood	Steel	Masonry
400	20mm (¾in)	8mm (⁵⁄₁₆in)	10mm (⅜in)
450	20mm (¾in)	10mm (⅜in)	13mm (½in)
550	25mm (1in)	10mm (⅜in)	15mm (⁹⁄₁₆in)
650	40mm (1½in)	13mm (½in)	20mm (¾in)

Cordless drills are powered by a battery fitted in the handle, which has to be recharged from time to time. Generally the recharging time is one hour, and the more expensive drills come with two batteries so that you can have one in use and one on charge.

There are three battery voltages: 7.2 volts for light, occasional use; 9.6 volts for normal woodworking; and 12 volts for heavy duty. Of course, the greater the power, the greater the cost, and in any case the cheapest models cost roughly double the price of an equivalent mains-powered drill.

The drills have the same extra facilities as their mains-powered counterparts, except that the hammer action is only available on the most expensive models.

JIGS AND TECHNIQUES FOR BANDSAWS

1 BEVELLING ON THE BANDSAW

When the table is set at the angle required for bevelling, the workpiece will often tend to slide off. This can be avoided by cramping a fence across below the saw blade, as shown. Make sure that the guard can still be positioned so that it does not foul the workpiece.

2 CUTTING DISCS ON THE BANDSAW

This simple jig works very effectively and enables you to cut discs of varying diameters. It is straightforward to make and consists of a baseboard cramped to the bandsaw table, plus a sliding arm which can be adjusted to give the required disc diameter.

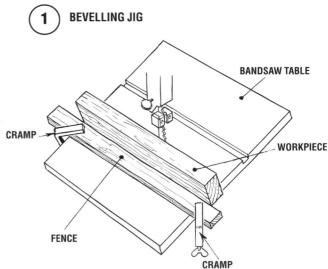

1 BEVELLING JIG

BANDSAW TABLE

WORKPIECE

CRAMP

FENCE

CRAMP

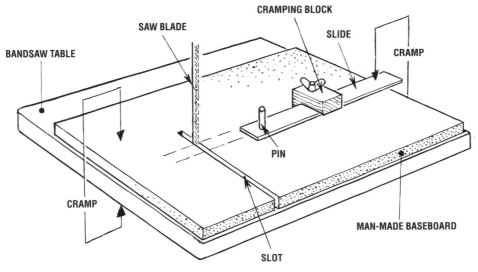

2 DISC-CUTTING JIG

SAW BLADE

CRAMPING BLOCK

SLIDE

CRAMP

BANDSAW TABLE

PIN

CRAMP

MAN-MADE BASEBOARD

SLOT

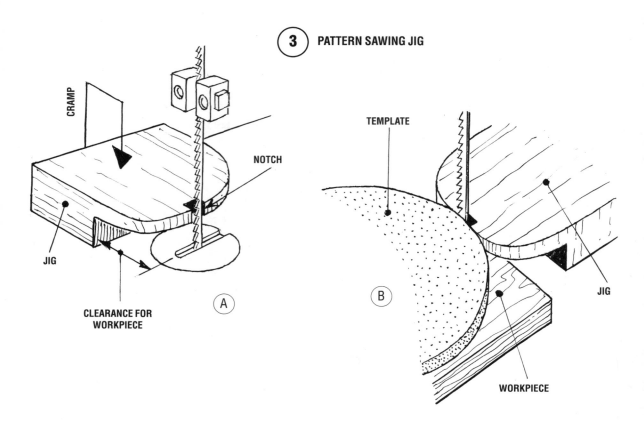

(3) **PATTERN SAWING JIG**

A hole is drilled in the baseboard and through the cramping block and a bolt is inserted to hold them together, secured by a wing nut. The bolt should have a countersunk head to fit into a corresponding countersinking on the baseboard so that the whole thing sits flat on the table.

The workpiece has a small hole drilled through its centre which fits snugly over a pivot pin (which can be a nail with its end nipped off). It is important that the pin is 10mm (⅜in) or so in front of the bandsaw blade, as shown by the dotted line, to allow for a slight lead-in.

3 PATTERN SAWING ON THE BANDSAW

This simple jig is indispensable when cutting shapes with converse and convex curves. An oval shape is a good example and is used here to illustrate the jig.

Note the space left to accommodate the size of the workpiece, and the notch in the rounded nose of the fence, which has to be made carefully to allow the blade enough space to run freely and to stand clear of the edges of the notch by its own thickness: it will then be able to follow the template shape accurately. It would be worthwhile making several jigs to suit different thicknesses of workpiece.

4 COILING A BANDSAW

The technique shown here for coiling a small bandsaw involves three stages.

First, grip the saw blade firmly at opposite sides with the back of your right hand (or left

(4) COILING THE BANDSAW

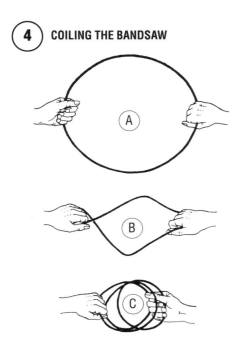

hand if you are left-handed) facing you (**fig A**). Twist your hands in opposite directions, one towards and the other away from you, at the same time letting them come closer together (**fig B**). The blade should then spring into a triple coil (**fig C**).

5 CROSSCUTTING ON THE SAWBENCH

An effective device for crosscutting lengths of wood square is illustrated in **fig A**.

A piece of 16mm (⅝in) MDF is screwed to a strip of metal, hardwood or rigid plastic, which must be a sliding fit in the channel of the saw table. A fence is also screwed to the MDF and should be of such a height as not to foul the crown guard. A small stop block can be cramped to the fence for repetiton work.

In a similar way, the multi-angle device (shown in **fig 11** on page 151) can be adapted to cut mitres on a sawbench by altering the thickness of the blade so that it runs smoothly in the channel on the saw table. **Fig B** is a plan view of the general arrangement.

6 TAPER CUTTING ON THE SAWBENCH

This is one of the most useful jigs you can make, as cutting tapers is a job that often needs to be done safely and accurately, and this design meets both requirements.

Fig A overleaf shows how it is made from two

(5) CROSSCUTTING DEVICE

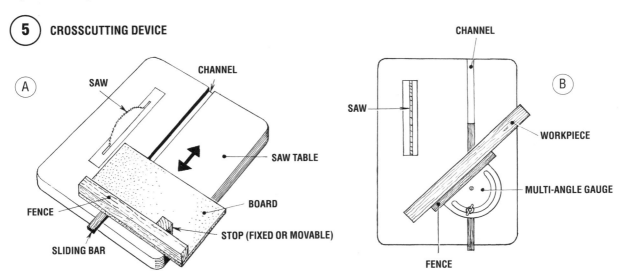

6 TAPER CUTTING JIG

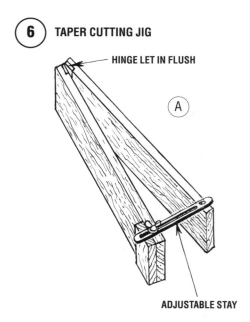

HINGE LET IN FLUSH

(A)

ADJUSTABLE STAY

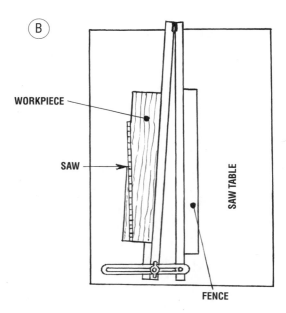

(B)

WORKPIECE

SAW

SAW TABLE

FENCE

long strips of wood hinged together. The strips could be 45 x 19mm (1¾ x ¾in) and whatever length suits your sawbench or the work in hand. The leaves of the hinge are recessed so that the strips close flush on each other; an ordinary straight cabinet stay provides the adjustment and a stop is positioned as shown. Use a dowel screw and wing nut to tighten down the stay.

The way in which the jig works in practice is shown in plan view in **fig B**, where a tapered leg is being sawn.

7 DEFLECTING GUARD ON THE SAWBENCH

When sawing small items, one of the most unnerving experiences is to have an offcut shoot at you at the speed of a bullet. This happens when the offcut is caught between the rising saw teeth and the riving knife, and jams there until the teeth eventually throw it back – at you!

In this plan view of a saw table, a wooden guard shaped like a finger, which tapers down to a feather edge, is cramped to the edge of the table in such a way that the feather edge just brushes the saw in front of the riving knife, so that the offcuts are deflected away safely.

When cutting off small pieces it is essential to hold the material by means of a jig like the one shown, which slides against the fence.

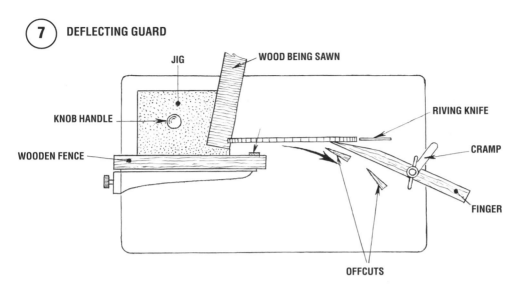

7 DEFLECTING GUARD

JIG

WOOD BEING SAWN

KNOB HANDLE

RIVING KNIFE

WOODEN FENCE

CRAMP

FINGER

OFFCUTS

JIGS FOR THE SAWBENCH

1 CUTTING TENONS I

With this jig, the workpiece is held vertically by hand in a push block, which has a guide attached at the front to hold it in position. Many sawbenches have a fence that is too low to keep the workpiece upright, which is obviously essential for both safety and accuracy, and it is well worthwhile screwing a thicker and deeper wooden one to the fence supplied with the machine.

The great advantage of this jig is that it can be put together so quickly that it is no great hardship to make individual ones to suit any particular job. The disadvantage is that you cannot leave the crown guard in place while working, and this is not to be recommended from the point of view of safety.

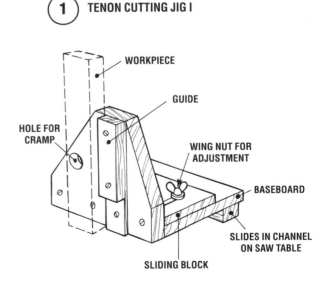

1 TENON CUTTING JIG I

WORKPIECE

GUIDE

HOLE FOR
CRAMP

WING NUT FOR
ADJUSTMENT

BASEBOARD

SLIDES IN CHANNEL
ON SAW TABLE

SLIDING BLOCK

2 CUTTING TENONS II

This is a safer design. Here, the workpiece is thumb-cramped as shown to the sloping jig, which could be made from 16mm (⅝in) MDF. Note the slot for the cramp: when working, the latter can be used as one hand-hold while the other hand pushes – the jig is automatically held upright. If you wish, a small stop can be screwed to the bottom edge of the back, so that it will catch the edge of the saw table and stop the jig going any further; or, the jig can be made to ride in the channel in the saw table as shown.

The work can be done with the crown guard in place. The bottom ends of the sawcuts will necessarily be curved slightly from the periphery of the saw teeth, but this imperfec-

tion will of course be removed when you cut the shoulders.

3 CUTTING TENONS III

This set-up takes into account the fact that at least eight cuts are necessary to make a tenon, and any jig that helps to make them safely and accurately is obviously worthwhile. Although this device holds the workpiece vertically, it can also be adjusted to hold it at any angle when angled tenons are required, as often happens in chair work. The jig shown is for use on the left-hand side of the saw, but it can equally well be made to operate from the opposite side.

The baseboard is fixed to a slide bar which must run freely along the channel in the saw

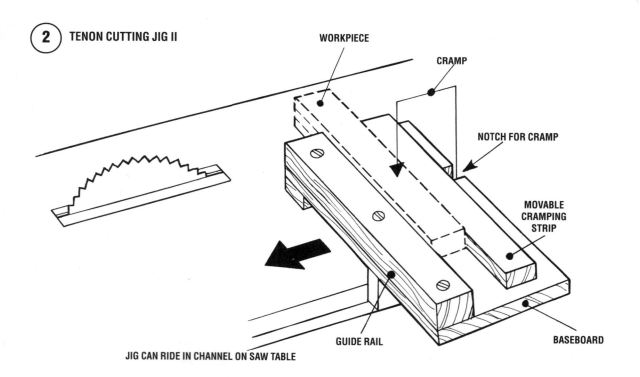

2 TENON CUTTING JIG II

WORKPIECE

CRAMP

NOTCH FOR CRAMP

MOVABLE CRAMPING STRIP

BASEBOARD

GUIDE RAIL

JIG CAN RIDE IN CHANNEL ON SAW TABLE

3 **TENON CUTTING JIG III**

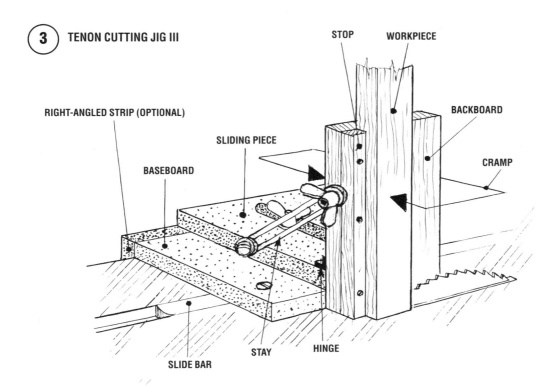

STOP

WORKPIECE

RIGHT-ANGLED STRIP (OPTIONAL)

BACKBOARD

SLIDING PIECE

BASEBOARD

CRAMP

STAY

HINGE

SLIDE BAR

table; a right-angled strip can be screwed to the back edge of the baseboard if desired to help as an auxiliary guide, but it is not essential. A sliding piece is mounted on the baseboard and has a slot cut in it, through which a bolt and wing nut are fitted so that it can be moved closer to or further from the saw blade.

A backboard is hinged to the sliding piece so that it can be tilted at an angle and is fixed by means of a bolt and wing nut running in a stay. The backboard also has a stop screwed to it for the workpiece to butt against, and the workpiece itself is cramped very firmly to the backboard.

MISCELLANEOUS ACCESSORIES

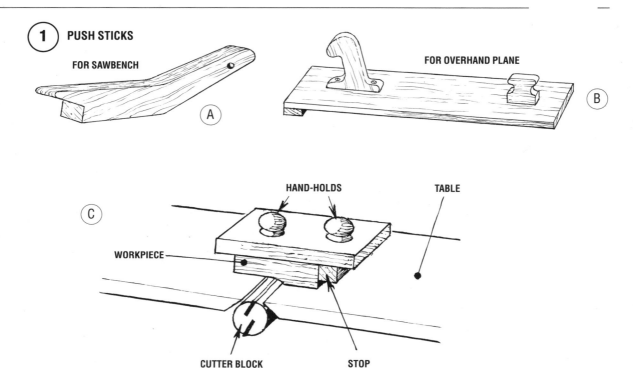

1 **PUSH STICKS**

FOR SAWBENCH

FOR OVERHAND PLANE

A

B

C

HAND-HOLDS

TABLE

WORKPIECE

CUTTER BLOCK

STOP

1 PUSH STICKS

It is all too easy to grab the nearest piece of scrapwood to save one's fingers when passing work through a sawbench. There is no standard design for a push stick, but the one shown in **fig A** is simple to make and offers a safe and effective accessory; two or three could be made and hung within easy reach.

Fig B shows a pusher for holding work safely on an overhand plane. It is intended for comparatively large workpieces and it would be easy to make a smaller one along the same lines.

Also for use on an overhand plane, the push block shown in **fig C** allows you to plane short lengths, which can otherwise be a dangerous business. It does involve removing the bridge guard, but the push block itself provides protection against the hazards of snatching or throwback.

2 MITRE SHOOTING BOARD

This is especially useful if you have a power plane, as the workpiece is cramped in position instead of being held by hand and this means you can devote both your hands to directing the plane.

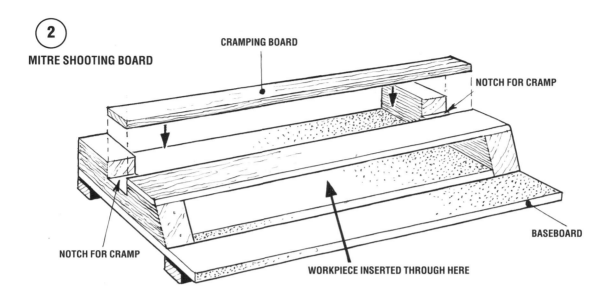

② **MITRE SHOOTING BOARD**

CRAMPING BOARD

NOTCH FOR CRAMP

NOTCH FOR CRAMP

BASEBOARD

WORKPIECE INSERTED THROUGH HERE

The device shown here is straightforward enough to make, but there are one or two points to watch. First, the whole thing is raised on four blocks, one at each corner, so that you can put the arm of your G- or thumb cramp underneath. Second, the baseboard must be wide enough to provide a ledge for your plane to slide on. Finally, the slots should accept the cramping board as a sliding fit and should be sufficiently deep to accommodate the thickest workpiece you are likely to use.

3 PLANING VENEER IN A THICKNESSER
Also called a 'panel planer', this type of machine used to be restricted to factories but smaller versions suitable for home workshops have now been on the market for some time.

The machine can be used to plane veneers, which should be laid on a stout baseboard – perhaps a piece of 19mm (¾in) chipboard which should be 200mm (8in) or so larger all round ·than the veneer. This works well, provided that

the veneer lies perfectly flat and its leading edge can be picked up by the feed roller. However, if the edge is split or buckled the roller will seize on it and tear the lot to shreds.

To prevent this from happening, cut a wide, shallow trench across the chipboard at the leading end and gently bend the veneer down into it, pinning it if necessary.

③ **VENEER PLANING SET-UP**

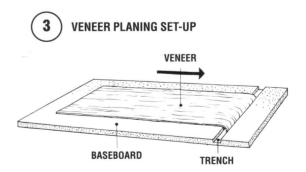

VENEER

BASEBOARD

TRENCH

(4) **DISC TRUING SET-UP**

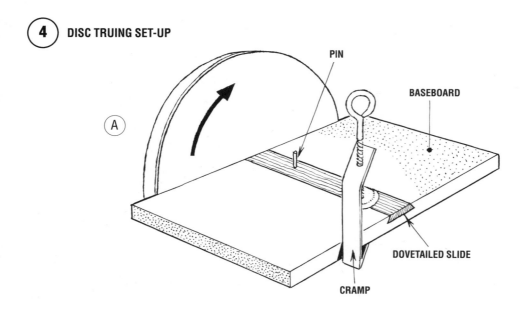

PIN

BASEBOARD

A

DOVETAILED SLIDE

CRAMP

4 TRUING DISCS ON A SANDER

Figs A and **B** show a useful set-up for truing discs which have been sawn roughly to shape by means of a jigsaw or bandsaw.

The job is done using a disc sander which has a baseboard (ply, MDF or chipboard) cramped to its existing table. The baseboard has a dovetailed slide fitted into it, which has a pin or cut-off nail with the point protruding driven through it at a convenient distance from the sander – 50mm (2in) would be suitable in most cases. The centre hole of the disc to be trued up is placed over the pin and the slide pushes it against the sander. The slide is cramped in place as shown; the cramp can also hold the whole jig tightly on the table.

Note that only the shaded quadrant on the face of the sander can be used for this kind of work, as its rotation helps to force the disc down on to the pivot pin.

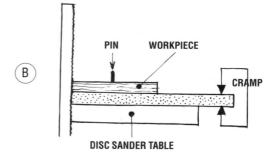

PIN   WORKPIECE

B

CRAMP

DISC SANDER TABLE

Chapter *4*

JIGS, ACCESSORIES AND TECHNIQUES FOR POWER ROUTERS

The portable plunge router was introduced in the 1950s and it has become increasingly popular since the incorporation of the 'plunging' facility in the 1980s. This allows the woodworker to position the router directly on to the work and, after adjusting the cutter to the correct depth, press down on two handles to start the machine and make the cut.

There are very few jobs the router cannot do, particularly if it is used in conjunction with a jig of some kind, many of which you can make yourself. This chapter is concerned mainly with the design of these jigs and how they work. First, however, there are a few basic principles which must be observed:

- Do not over-tighten the collet on to the cutter as this can create grooves or distort the collet, resulting in a poor finish.
- Make sure you are cutting in the right direction by feeding the router in the opposite direction to the rotation of the cutter, as shown in **fig 1**.
- It is impossible to quote definite recommendations for cutting speeds, because these vary according to the kind of wood being cut, the diameter of the cutter and the intricacy of the design. A ¼in diameter cutter normally needs a speed between 20,000rpm and 24,000rpm, while a ¾in diameter cutter needs between 14,000rpm and 20,000rpm.
- Running the router at too low a speed can result in the wood being burned, and the obvious remedy is to increase the speed. There are occasions, however, when sharp curves or bends, or a difficult pattern can only be negotiated at a slow speed, and a good tip is to adjust the cutting depths so that

1   **ROUTER CUTTING DIRECTIONS**

FIRST CUT

SECOND CUT

THIRD CUT

FOURTH CUT

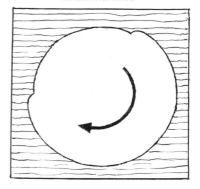

INNER PROFILING

the last cut is a light skim which will remove the burn marks. As an example, if you have to make a 12mm (½in) deep cut, try making one 10mm (⅜in) deep plus a finishing cut of 2mm (¹⁄₁₆in) to remove the burn mark.

MODES OF USE

The router is so versatile that the best way to learn about the jobs it can do is to buy a book or subscribe to a magazine specializing in the subject, which is too complicated to be dealt with fully here. Not all woodworkers are aware of the full scope of the machine: **fig 2** shows the four principal modes in diagrammatic form, and the manufacturers have been quick to introduce special kits allowing the router to be mounted in each of them.

Fig A shows the standard or basic mode of use, where the router is moved over a fixed workpiece.

Fig B shows the mode in which the router is inverted and held rigid by a proprietary device which allows it to be used like a spindle moulder. This means that you can work mouldings or make several kinds of joints: a design you can make in the workshop is included on page 58.

In **fig C**, the router is fixed in an upright position and the workpiece is fastened temporarily to a template which is moved over and directed by a guide pin: again, several manufacturers offer the necessary accessories.

Finally, **fig D** shows a situation where the router moves and the workpiece is fixed, the movement of the router being guided by horizontal rails. An arrangement of this kind that you can make for yourself is explained on page 60.

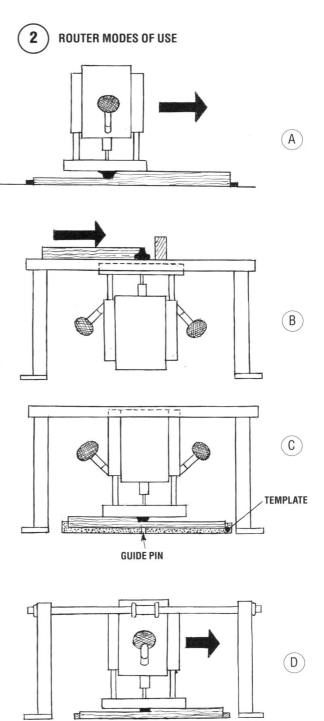

2 ROUTER MODES OF USE

A

B

C

TEMPLATE

GUIDE PIN

D

ACCESSORIES AND CUTTERS

When you buy a router, you will find that it comes with several accessories such as guide fences, a trammel, special bushes and fine-adjustment devices. And it will not be long before you will have to buy such things as guide bushes, collars and bearings of various sizes, and if you wish to cut dovetail joints there are special kits available.

You will also need a catalogue showing the wide range of cutters on offer – the number must run into hundreds. For home workshop use they are made in three grades: HSS (high-speed steel); TCT (tungsten-carbide tipped); and TC (solid tungsten carbide). Cutters made from HSS are suitable only for light or for intermittent work on natural timber, and although they can give a fine finish at first they will blunt very quickly, particularly on man-made boards. TCT cutters are the most popular, and although expensive will outlast HSS many times over by virtue of the fact that the cutting surfaces are made from tungsten carbide welded to the body. TC cutters are more expensive still and are used mainly for work that requires heavy cutters.

The rest of this chapter is devoted to explaining some of the many jigs and accessories you can make for yourself, often from materials which would otherwise be scrapped. In many cases, it is impossible to give exact sizes as they will vary according to the design of the router itself, but the important thing is to understand the principle on which the jig works rather than to copy its precise dimensions.

JIGS AND ACCESSORIES FOR POWER ROUTERS

1 AVOIDING SPLITS AT CORNERS

Splitting out at corners is more likely to happen when trimming a piece of natural wood rather than a man-made board, and the simplest way to avoid it is by adopting the method shown in **fig 1** on page 48. Any splits that result from cutting across the grain will be removed when cutting along it. An alternative method is to cramp pieces of scrap wood tightly alongside the workpiece so that any splits are transferred to them.

2 BASE PLATE EXTENSION FOR EDGE TRIMMING

It is sometimes necessary to make a heavy cut on the edge of a workpiece and this can make it difficult to prevent the router from subsequently tilting over.

A base plate extension can be made easily in the workshop to suit a particular job. Some router manufacturers provide threaded holes in the base plate which allow a device like this

to be screwed on; otherwise, it can be fixed on with double-sided adhesive tape. The extension can be made from scrap offcuts, but it is important to bear in mind that its thickness has to be deducted from the depth of cut, so it should be as thin as possible without being too weak to do the job.

3 SKI ATTACHMENT

This is an easily made device which will prove to be invaluable when the surface of a comparatively large workpiece needs to be routed flat, or when a piece of delicate carving or pierced work has to be machined and it is desirable that the router itself should not come into direct contact with it.

The ski strips shown overleaf are two long strips of equal length with holes drilled so that they will slide along the guide rods. You must obviously be able to hold them in a fixed position, and for this you will need to drill a

 BASE PLATE EXTENSION

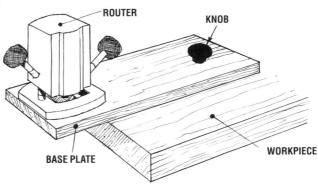

ROUTER

KNOB

BASE PLATE

WORKPIECE

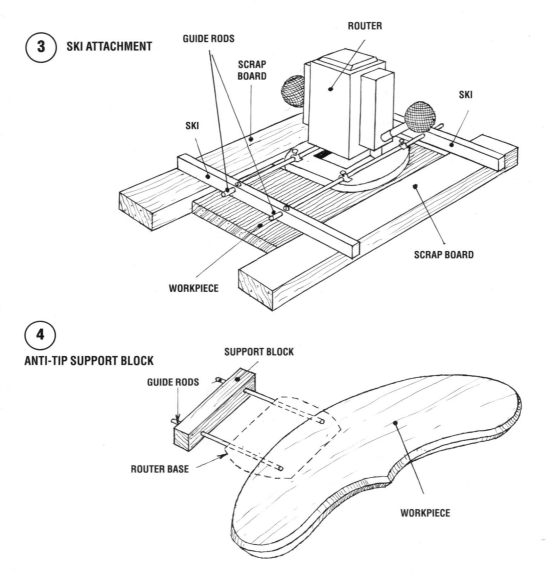

③ SKI ATTACHMENT

GUIDE RODS

ROUTER

SCRAP BOARD

SKI

SKI

WORKPIECE

SCRAP BOARD

④

ANTI-TIP SUPPORT BLOCK

SUPPORT BLOCK

GUIDE RODS

ROUTER BASE

WORKPIECE

vertical hole downwards where a guide rod passes through a ski. The diameter of the hole should be such that you can hammer a tee-nut into it, and a matching bolt can be screwed into it to hold the ski and guide pin extremely firmly together.

The only other necessities are two large pieces of scrap board, which can be cramped, or held tightly against the workpiece. They must be the same thickness as each other and thick enough to make sure that neither the skis nor the router itself can touch the workpiece.

4 ANTI-TIP SUPPORT BLOCK

You will sometimes come across a situation where the edge of an awkwardly shaped workpiece cannot be moulded without the danger of the router tipping over.

To prevent this, the guide rods should be secured to the router as shown so that enough of their length protrudes to pass through holes in a support block, which must be of the correct thickness to hold the router level.

If you are going to use the device for a number of identical workpieces it would be worthwhile fixing the guide rods as explained for the ski attachment above, but if it is a 'one off' then the rods simply need to be a tight fit.

5 JIG FOR REPETITION WORK

This is a handy jig which allows you to rout individual pieces to the same pattern one after another, or to rout a 'repeat' design on a long workpiece at regular intervals. It could just as well be used to drill holes at a series of predetermined positions.

This jig basically consists of a tray with the pattern to be routed cut in a hinged lid. This is held tightly closed by hooks and eyes, arranged so that the lid presses down firmly on the workpiece.

5 **JIG FOR REPETITION WORK**

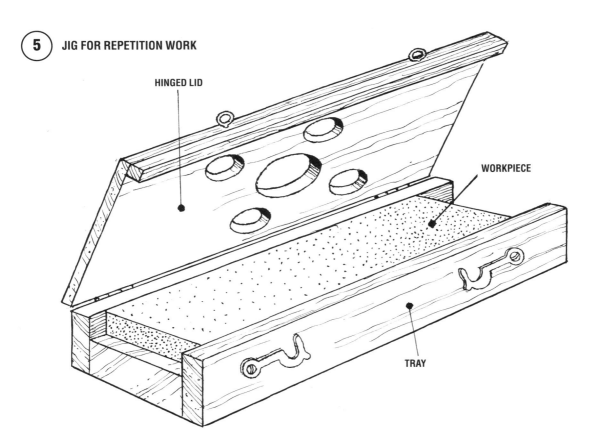

HINGED LID

WORKPIECE

TRAY

6 PARALLEL ROUTING JIG

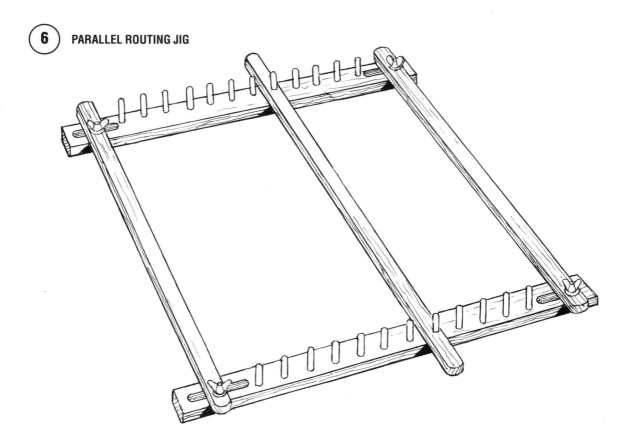

6 PARALLEL ROUTING JIG

This is a large adjustable jig for routing parallel grooves or channels on one or both sides of a workpiece. It would be possible to position the workpiece so that a diagonal pattern could be routed.

Dowel pegs are inserted as shown into holes drilled in two identical strips, ensuring that the pegs are equidistant and also exactly opposite each other. The distance between the pegs depends on the job you have to do but must obviously be enough to allow the lateral guide strips to be slotted over the pegs. Wing nuts which can be tightened down into slots make the jig adjustable.

7 HOLDING WORKPIECES WITHOUT CRAMPS

Double-sided adhesive tape is strongly recommended for this as, provided the surfaces are clean, dry and dust-free, it will hold the workpiece firmly on a bench or baseboard. When the job is finished, the tape can be peeled off easily.

A similar method involves using Velcro: this consists of two tapes which when pressed together will mesh with each other by means of the tiny hooks on one tape engaging with the loops on the other. The tape is available in various widths and is backed with adhesive so that it can be stuck down. It resists sideways and downwards pressure surprisingly strongly, yet the strips can still be peeled apart and reused.

Also available (from the Axminster Power Tool Centre – see Suppliers) is a router mat made of flexible rubber which can be placed on a bench and will hold the workpiece down with no danger of slipping.

8 HOLDING BOARD

The power router is one of the most versatile tools in the workshop and is satisfying to use as well. It is therefore annoying to find its use restricted by the several cramps that are normally needed to hold the workpiece steady on the bench.

The board shown in **fig A** will overcome this difficulty as the workpiece is held by eccentrically shaped cams, as shown in **fig B**. To make the set-up, you need a baseboard which should be the width of your bench by, say, 610mm (24in) long; the sizes can be varied to suit the circumstances, but it is a good idea to have it larger rather than smaller. A piece of 16mm (⅝in) white plastic-faced board would be ideal, but any smooth board would suffice.

Mark off a grid of 75mm (3in) squares over the entire surface and use the intersections as centres for 10mm (⅜in) holes, which should be perfectly vertical and drilled right through. Make the cams from 10mm (⅜in) plywood to the shape shown in **fig B**, and drill a 10mm (⅜in) hole eccentrically; then glue the same diameter of dowel, 13mm (½in) long, into the hole. To ensure a good fixing, which is essential, it is a good idea to run one end of the dowel along some saw teeth to form a slot and then tap in a tiny wedge to force the sides apart.

You may have to ease the dowels on the cams by glasspapering them lightly so that they are a sliding fit in the holes on the baseboard – lubricating them with the end of a candle will also help.

There is no need to make a cam for every hole as six should be sufficient to hold any workpiece, even if it is an awkward shape. Remember that the thickness of the cam must always be less than that of the workpiece.

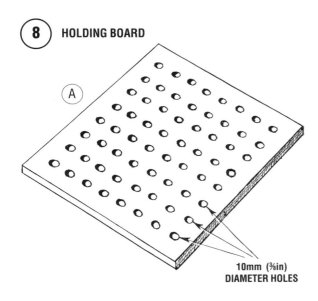

8 HOLDING BOARD

(A)

10mm (⅜in)
DIAMETER HOLES

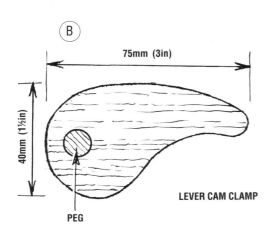

(B)

75mm (3in)

40mm (1½in)

LEVER CAM CLAMP

PEG

9 ROUTING SMALL PIECES

Figs A and **B** show how this jig can be held in a vice; its primary use is to groove a quantity of small pieces, and as it can be made very easily from small offcuts of wood or man-made board it can be made up for a single job and then discarded.

The jig consists of two lining blocks, inner and outer, the latter having a bearer fixed to it at right angles. This is shown in **fig A** and again in **fig B**, where you can see how the router is positioned with its fence riding against the edge of the outer bearer, which acts as a guide.

10 ROUTING LONG DOVETAILS

The set-up shown in **figs A** and **B** opposite can be used to rout a long dovetail along the end of a rail. The arrangement can be adapted to cut similar dovetails along the edges of panels made from man-made boards, as in a set of shelves where the dovetails would fit into matching slots.

Fig A shows the set-up, which can be held in a vice or between the jaws of a Workmate. From **fig B**, you will see that two passes with the router are needed to shape the dovetail. The workpiece is held between two blocks which

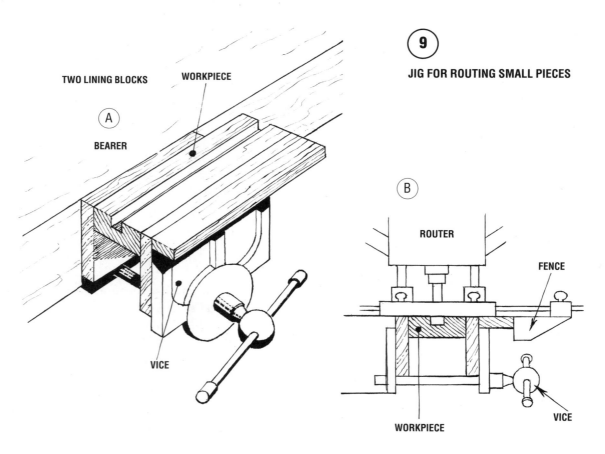

TWO LINING BLOCKS   WORKPIECE

A

BEARER

VICE

9

JIG FOR ROUTING SMALL PIECES

B

ROUTER

FENCE

WORKPIECE

VICE

have bearers screwed to them – it is important that the screws are located well back from the edges, as it may be necessary to cut into the bearers to form the dovetail.

11 MAKING AND USING TEMPLATES

When using a template, you will need to fit a guide bush to the base of your router. This is simply a special collar that can be screwed into place easily and its purpose is to ensure that the cutter travels smoothly and easily around the shape of the template.

The way it works is shown in profile overleaf, and from this you will see that an allowance **e** has to be made for the diameter of the guide bush. To calculate it, deduct the cutter diameter **x** from that of the guide bush **y** and halve it: in other words, $e = \frac{1}{2}(y-x)$.

To make a template, draw the exact shape on to thin card or stout paper, draw another line outside the first, following it exactly, and cut your template to this outer line.

Templates can be cut from several materials, but whichever you use it should be between 6mm and 10mm (¼in and ⅜in) thick. If the template is to be used only a few times you could use hardboard though MDF would be better, while for templates which are going to be subjected to hard use it would be advisable to use Tufnol, a material made specially for the job. It is available from wood centres (in case of difficulty, contact Trend – see Suppliers).

10 JIG FOR MAKING LONG DOVETAILS

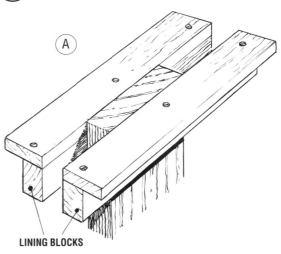

LINING BLOCKS

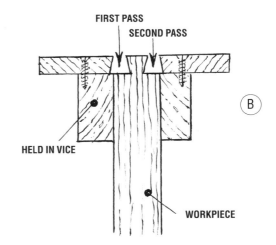

FIRST PASS
SECOND PASS
HELD IN VICE
WORKPIECE

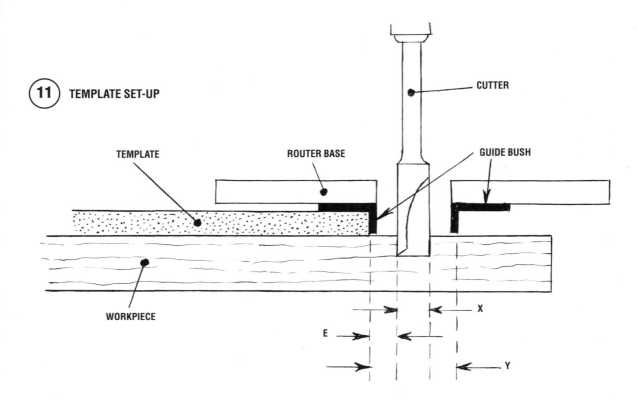

11 TEMPLATE SET-UP

CUTTER

TEMPLATE

ROUTER BASE

GUIDE BUSH

WORKPIECE

X

E

Y

12 MAKING A ROUTER TABLE

Router tables are used with the router invert-ed so the cutter protrudes through a hole in the table (in a similar way to a spindle moulder) and there are many designs on the market. Even so, many woodworkers prefer to make their own so that they can incorporate special features. The following description has to be general as routers vary in size and design, but it is usually only a matter of modifying the table slightly to accommodate any differences.

A handy size for the table would be 610 x 380mm (24 x 15in) and although you could use one piece of MDF 19mm (¾in) thick, it is bet-ter if it is made up of two pieces, each 10mm (⅜in) thick, screwed together, as this will help to eliminate vibration.

Fig A opposite shows a plan view. Note that there must be enough space behind the fences for them to be adjusted backwards or forwards, at the same time allowing you plenty of space on the working side.

A metal plate is fixed halfway along the length of the table, measuring 186mm (7³⁄₁₆in) square by 3.2mm (⅛in) thick. It is drilled with sets of holes so that it can be screwed to the bases of most makes of routers, and to the table itself once you have routed out a 3.2mm deep recess for it to drop into. You will also have to cut a hole right through the table to match the one on the plate, through which the cutter can protrude. (In case of difficulty, this plate is avail-able from Trend – see Suppliers. They can also supply a levelling kit to ensure that the plate

12 ROUTER TABLE

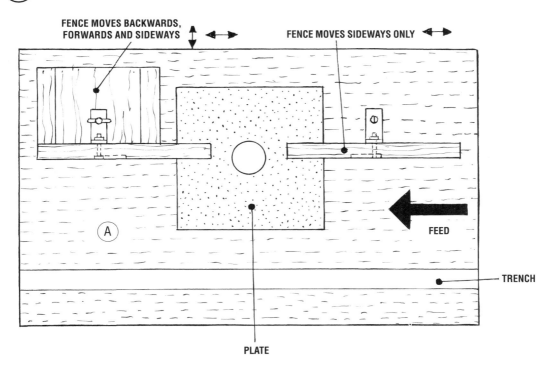

FENCE MOVES BACKWARDS, FORWARDS AND SIDEWAYS

FENCE MOVES SIDEWAYS ONLY

FEED

TRENCH

A

PLATE

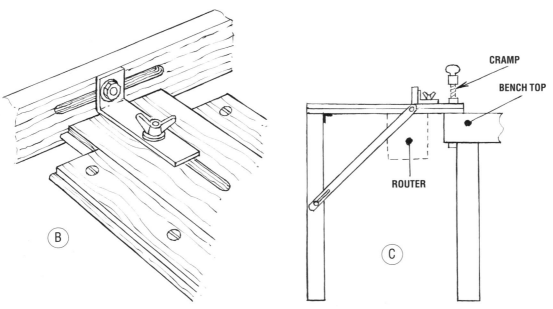

B

CRAMP

BENCH TOP

ROUTER

C

and surrounding wood are absolutely flat and flush with each other.)

You can make one of these plates yourself if you have simple metalworking facilities; the holes can then be drilled to suit the base of your router – the central hole needs to be large enough to accept the biggest cutter you will be using.

The fences are straightforward to make, bearing in mind that the leaving fence has to be adjustable so that it can be moved backwards or forwards to compensate for any wood removed from the workpiece during machining. A suitable fence is shown in **fig B** on the previous page and consists of a short length of ordinary tongued and grooved boarding which slides between narrow strips of the same kind of board. It has a slot cut through it centrally which accepts a bolt that protrudes through the top and the slide, and is held in place by the usual washer and wing nut. A right-angled bracket or block holds the slide and fence together. Both fences have a short slot cut longitudinally in their faces through which a coach bolt is inserted, so that they can be moved sideways as required.

You can purchase an adjustable fence with a built-in cowl and spout for dust extraction, or a dust extraction cowl on its own, and this is so reasonably priced that it really is not worth making one up for yourself. (Again, in case of difficulty contact Trend – see Suppliers.)

Fig A shows a trench routed along the length of the table at a convenient distance from the fence, and this accepts a sliding cross-fence which holds workpieces against the fence and ensures that everything is square.

When working small mouldings you will need to protect your fingers; the mouldings can be fixed temporarily with double-sided adhesive tape to a larger block of wood, which you can hold easily.

You can, of course, make up a frame with legs so that the table is free-standing, or you can fit it with fold-up legs which support it at one end, the other end being cramped to your bench, as in **fig C**. In my own case, I found that the Elu MOF96 fitted neatly under the open jaws of my Workmate.

13 MULTI-PURPOSE JIG

The idea for this jig had been in my mind for a long time before I got round to making the basic framework, but before I could put the final touches to it and find out what it could do, I was taken ill. A friend and neighbour, David Beard, came to my rescue by finishing and experimenting with it, and both he and I were surprised at its versatility.

Making the jig Apart from the drawer slides, which cost very little, the rest of the parts can be made up from offcuts and everyday hardware. The dimensions shown are for guidance only, as the model and size of your router will determine most of them; the one used here is the popular Elu MOF96E.

The router is supported on its fence guide rods and this allows it to be moved transversely along them, the working distance being 115mm (4½in); it can, of course, be held at any position along them by tightening the thumb screws. The ends of the rods are housed in holes drilled in two 19 x 19mm (¾ x ¾in) wood strips and small bolts are tightened down into tee-nuts to make sure they cannot move. The wood strips are screwed to the moving part of the drawer slide – making the necessary holes is quite simple, as the slides are made of aluminium alloy which can be drilled easily. You

13 MULTI-PURPOSE JIG

MAKING THE JIG

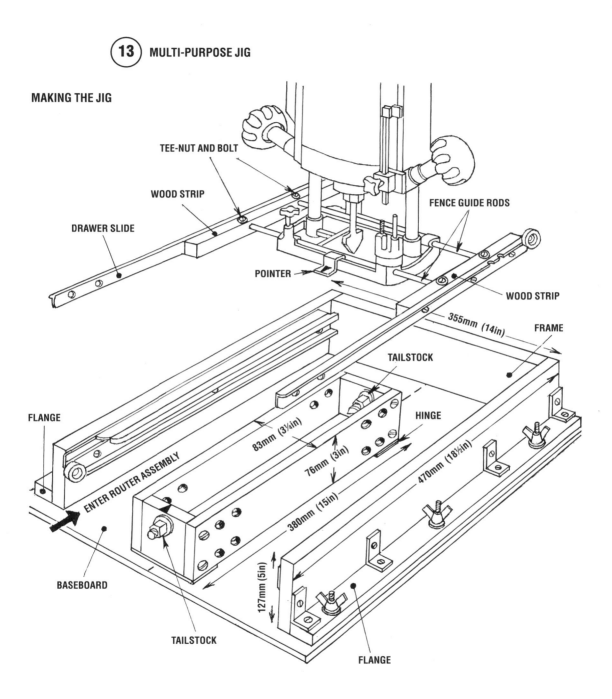

TEE-NUT AND BOLT

WOOD STRIP

DRAWER SLIDE

FENCE GUIDE RODS

POINTER

WOOD STRIP

355mm (14in)

FRAME

TAILSTOCK

FLANGE

83mm (3¼in)

HINGE

ENTER ROUTER ASSEMBLY

76mm (3in)

470mm (18½in)

380mm (15in)

BASEBOARD

127mm (5in)

TAILSTOCK

FLANGE

will need the side-fixing rather than bottom-fixing type of rod.

This completes the sub-assembly, apart from fixing a small pointer exactly halfway across the sole-plate of the router so that it is immediately in front of and in line with any cutter which is being used, and can therefore be employed as a guide and/or register mark.

Next comes the frame, which is made from 15mm (⅝in) particle board and could be chipboard or MDF. Its width is determined by the length of the guide rods plus the slides; its length is 470mm (18½in) and this allows the router to travel to the front of the frame – it can be altered to suit your requirements. By a happy chance, the width comes out at 355mm (14in) and this, once the flanges have been fixed on, enables the whole thing to sit comfortably on a Workmate, with the flanges cramped to it.

The fixed parts of the drawer slides are screwed onto their wood strips in the same way as the sliding parts are to theirs. But a word of warning: the screws must be well countersunk so that the screw heads do not foul each other when the jig is in operation.

The baseboard is, once again, made from particle board and it can be thinner than the frame at 10mm (⅜in). It can be fixed to the frame when required by means of bolts and wing nuts, and it is 12mm (½in) or so bigger all round than the frame. The important point is that when the two parts are fixed together the frame must be centred on the centre line of the baseboard.

The cradle, in a way an optional extra, but a very useful one, must be aligned along the centre line on the baseboard. It is a long shallow box with an open top and is made from 10mm (⅜in) ply or MDF; the sizes shown allow it to accommodate a block or cylinder just over

51mm (2in) square/in diameter and up to 330mm (13in) long. Note that a hinge is fitted at one end with a packing piece of the same thickness at the other end to keep it level. If the cradle is raised a bit at the unhinged end and a wedge inserted under it, you will be able to rout flutes or reeds that diminish along their length and eventually run out, as shown in **fig B** opposite. Both cradle ends are loose and can be held in any one of three positions by means of holes drilled through the sides, so that loose bolts can be inserted into holes drilled into the ends.

If you intend to use the cradle for working on turned blanks as well as square blocks, the two simplified tailstocks shown are indispensable. They are straightforward enough – just two bolts, with the ends ground to points, held in place by nuts, bolts and washers. Their height in the ends depends on the length of the shank of the cutter you will be using. A register mark made on the end of the cradle will help when you are routing flutes or reeds at regular intervals around the cylinder.

Using the jig The jig can be operated in three separate modes.

First, with the router assembly mounted on the frame and without the baseboard, the jig can be used in conjunction with the jaws of your Workmate or bench vice to cut dovetailed or tenon joints, as shown in **figs E** and **F**, or finger joints.

Routing the dovetails for a dovetailed joint is straightforward, as the workpiece can be held vertically in the jaws of a Workmate or bench vice and the router pulled forward to make the cuts. Cutting the sockets is more difficult, as the router cutter has to enter the workpiece end-on. The easiest way to achieve this is to use an

USING THE JIG

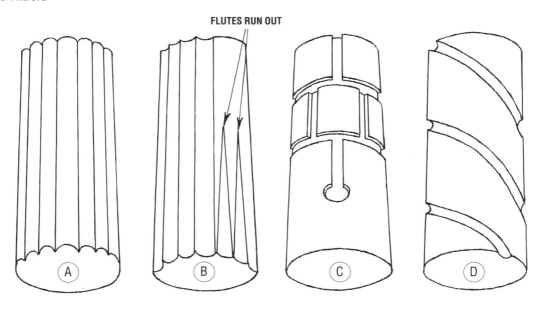

FLUTES RUN OUT

A   B   C   D

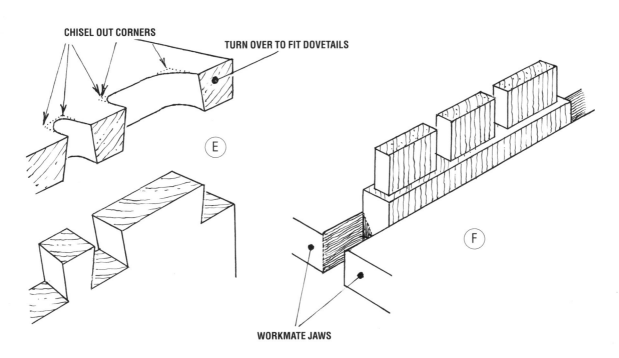

CHISEL OUT CORNERS

TURN OVER TO FIT DOVETAILS

E

F

WORKMATE JAWS

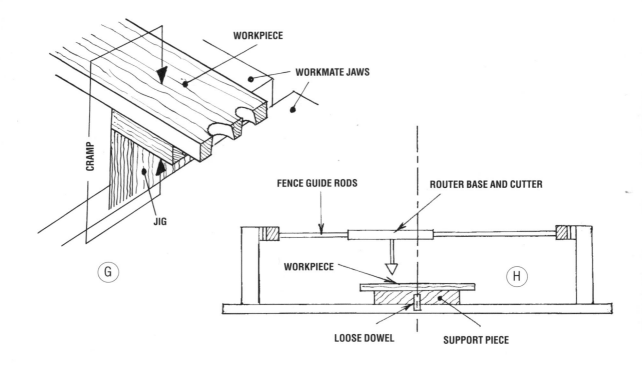

L-shaped jig to which the workpiece can be cramped, as shown in **fig G**. Even so, the cutter will leave rounded corners, as shown in **fig E**, and these will have to be chiselled out by hand or sawn out with a coping saw.

Second, when the baseboard is brought into use with the router assembly and the frame but without the cradle, a very useful job it can perform is to cut holes of any diameter in the workpiece, as shown in **fig H**. You will need to drill a hole through the baseboard at a convenient position on its centre line, into which a peg consisting of a short piece of 10mm (⅜in) dowel can be dropped. It should protrude by 6mm (¼in) or so, and a support piece of scrap wood with a matching hole is then placed over it – the whole thing must revolve freely and smoothly. The workpiece is then fitted to the support piece with double-sided adhesive tape. The router and cutter are moved sideways along the fence guide rods by a distance which is equal to the radius, so that when the router is started and plunged you will be able to turn the workpiece by hand to cut the hole.

In the same mode, you can undertake run-of-the-mill jobs such as grooving, rebating, recessing sunk panels and the like by fixing the workpieces to the baseboard temporarily with double-sided adhesive tape.

The third and last mode of use is with the cradle in position on the baseboard, a set-up which is of course indispensable when turned workpieces such as legs or columns have to be reeded or fluted.

A calculation has to be made in both cases as to how far the workpiece has to be moved round after routing each reed or flute. Let us suppose you have a cylindrical column on which you have to rout 20 reeds. The first step is to draw a circle of the same diameter as the workpiece on to a piece of paper. This circle contains 360 degrees into which is divided the number of reeds required – 20 – which means that each reed requires an angle of 18 degrees. Mark an 18 degree angle on your pencil drawing, and the distance this gives on the circumference is the amount the workpiece will have to be rotated for each reed, which can be measured off from the register mark shown on the cradle end in the set-up.

This is how the two cylinders in **figs A** and **B** on page 63 were worked; the diminishing flutes in **fig B** were accomplished by tilting the cradle very slightly. The lattice effect in **fig C** was made by moving the router up to the stops, which were small thumb cramps fixed on to the drawer slides. Believe it or not, the spiral in **fig D** was the easiest! The pitch depended on how quickly the router was moved by hand and it could be controlled by using one hand on the workpiece and the other on the router.

Here are two tips which may help you in this kind of work. First, if you pare down a pencil stub you can fix it into the router collet instead of a cutter, and then use it to make patterns on the workpiece that you can follow later with the cutter. Second, you may well find that when you are doing intricate work as in **fig C**, the cutter burns the wood and gives it a charred appearance. It is usually recommended that the router speed should be increased to prevent this from happening, but with complicated patterns it is often impossible to do this and the burning will still occur. The remedy is to arrange the depth of the last cut so that it is merely a light skim, which will take off just the burn marks.

Chapter 5

JIGS, ACCESSORIES AND TECHNIQUES FOR HAND WORK

As so many of the new generation of woodworkers are growing up with a limited knowledge of hand tools and techniques, this chapter begins by describing a good range of the tools most useful for home woodworking and their uses. Gluing is another job that must be done by hand, and so we also take a look at the range of adhesives available to today's woodworker. The remainder of the chapter is devoted to explaining a wide selection of jigs, devices and techniques for use in hand work.

HAND SAWS

Today, most saws are mass-produced, often with plastic handles and the new 'hardpoint' teeth, which can be recognized by their blue-black colour. These cannot be re-sharpened but remain sharp for four or five times longer than those cut in conventional steel; when the teeth become blunt, the whole saw is thrown away. Hardpoint saws are usually less than half the price of conventional saws so this is not as extravagant as it may seem, particularly when you bear in mind that they will cope easily with the abrasive nature of man-made boards which would ruin conventional carbon-steel teeth. If you spend a lot of time working with MDF, chipboard or plywood it would obviously be sensible to buy this kind of saw.

TRADITIONAL DESIGN

There are three kinds of traditional hand saw: the ripsaw, the crosscut saw and the panel saw.

The ripsaw is used for cutting along the grain, particularly in thicker wood, but as anyone who has tried it will tell you, it's a back-breaking and tiresome job even though the teeth are filed at right angles to the blade so that they cut easily. It is not surprising that portable power saws have now rendered the ripsaw almost obsolete.

The crosscut saw, as its name implies, is used to saw across the grain and has its teeth filed at an angle which is nominally 60 degrees for

1 **TRADITIONAL HAND SAW**

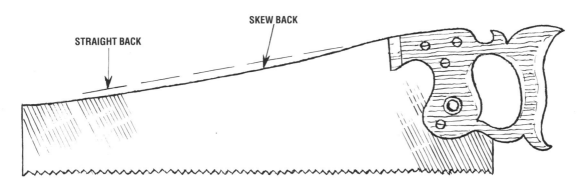

hardwood and 45 degrees for softwood, although the latter is the angle most commonly used. Again, this saw is fast being supplanted by power saws.

The more popular panel saw with hardpoint teeth is used for cutting joints and generally working standard sizes of timber, because it can function as both a ripsaw and a crosscut.

TENON SAW

The tenon saw, shown in **fig 2** is the largest member of the backsaw family, having blade lengths from 250mm to 355mm (10in to 14in), compared with the dovetail saw, from 200mm to 250mm (8in to 10in), and the gent's saw, from 125mm to 200mm (5in to 8in).

The tenon saw is the maid-of-all-work and no matter what new machines appear there will always be a use for it. As well as cutting tenons, it is used to saw battens, cut halved joints, trim ends, saw the larger sizes of dovetailed joints and do all the odd small sawing jobs for which it is not worth setting up a machine.

Backsaws are so called because they have a spine of either brass or steel folded over the back to make the blade more rigid and the whole saw weightier. In days gone by, the spine was invariably brass and the backsaw itself almost a work of art, with a beautifully shaped hardwood handle and brass screws holding this handle in place.

The greater the number of teeth per 25mm (1in), the finer the finish but the slower the cutting action; most tenon saws vary between 11 and 14 TPI (teeth-per-inch). Note that, alternatively, the number of teeth can be expressed as the number of points per inch (PPI), but there is always one extra point compared with the total number of teeth, so that 10 TPI is 11 PPI.

2 **TENON SAW**

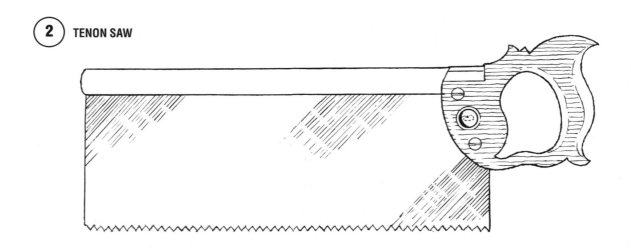

JAPANESE SAWS

The Japanese Ryoba saw, shown in **fig 3**, combines rip and crosscut functions on one blade, having teeth of each kind on opposite edges (the rip teeth increase in size along the blade from heel to toe). As with all Japanese saws, it cuts on the pull stroke instead of our traditional push stroke. The Japanese also produce hardpoint saws, namely the Hassunme ripsaw and a separate crosscut saw of the same name. The replaceable blades can be loosened by tapping them gently on a block of wood several times. When the new blade has been inserted, the back of the handle is tapped gently on the block to allow the blade to seat itself.

The Japanese Dozuki tenon saw, shown in **fig 4**, produces a fine clean cut and, like all Japanese saws, cuts on the pull stroke. The blade is 248mm (9¾in) long by 50mm (2in) deep, which obviously limits the depth of cut. There is also a hardpoint saw, the Ikedame, which has a blade 150mm (6in) long by 25mm

(1in) deep, and a larger one, the Doutsuki-Me, with a blade 240mm (9½in) long.

All Japanese saws have extremely small teeth, usually around 24 TPI, and this, together with their very thin blades, produces fine cuts and a clean finish. Cutting on the pull stroke eliminates any tendency of the blade to buckle, as would happen on the push stroke, and is logically a better method; it is said to have originated from the fact that Japanese craftsmen worked either sitting down or squatting, so that a long blade or a push stroke could not be used.

COPING SAWS

These useful little saws shown in **fig 5** overleaf, can be fitted with different blades, enabling them to cut metal and plastics as well as wood. Their great advantage is that the blade can be turned to cut at any angle. This can be utilized to cut dovetail sockets quickly, by first drilling a hole to remove most of the waste then sawing out the remainder.

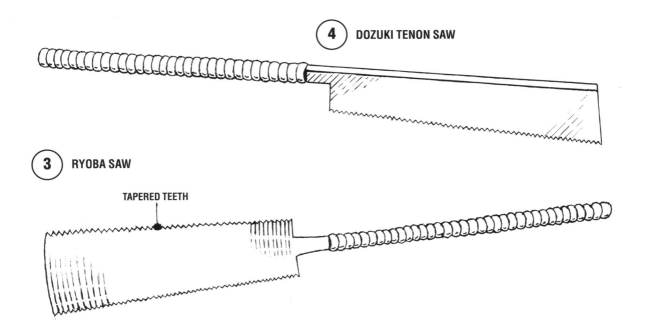

4 DOZUKI TENON SAW

3 RYOBA SAW

TAPERED TEETH

(5) COPING SAW

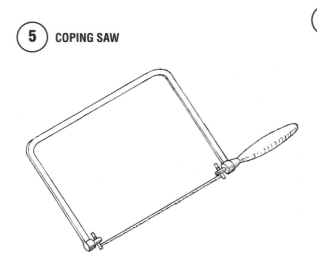

(6) CHISELS

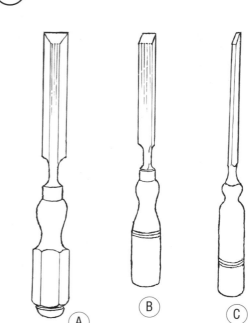

CHISELS

There are many designs of chisel, the three basic ones being shown in **fig 6**. The most popular is the bevelled edge design in **fig A** and this is particularly useful if you use a slicing cut, as shown in **fig 7**, which covers half as much area again and calls for a lower cutting angle, with consequently less effort required. The bevelled edges mean that the chisel can cut right up into the corners.

The firmer chisel shown in **fig B** is meant for heavier work and can be struck pretty firmly with a mallet; if you grind off the corners, as depicted in **fig 8**, it can be used to get into sharp corners.

Fig C shows the well-known mortise chisel, the 8mm (⁵⁄₁₆in) size being the most useful as it is about one-third the thickness of 22mm (⁷⁄₈in) stock, from which most rails are worked – the rule of thumb being that a tenon should be approximately one-third the thickness of the rail, with the mortise to match. If you can get a 3mm (⅛in) chisel, do so, as it is ideal for chopping out small dovetail sockets.

(7) USING A BEVELLED EDGE CHISEL

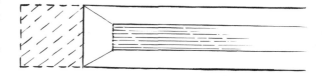

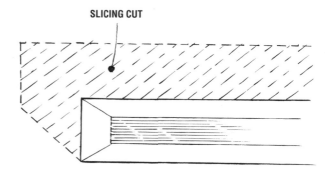

SLICING CUT

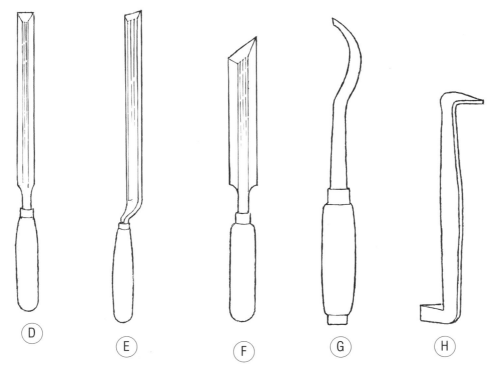

D E F G H

8 **CHISEL FOR SHARP CORNERS**

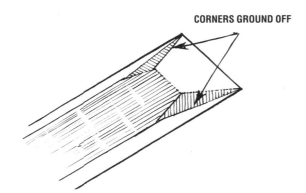

CORNERS GROUND OFF

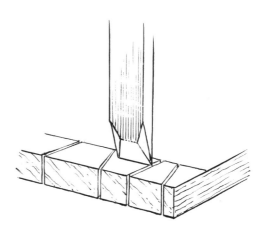

Another bevelled edge design is shown in **fig D** on the previous page which differs from that shown in **fig A** in being much longer and thinner, with the blade tapering towards the cutting edge. It is sacrilege to hit (or even lightly tap) one of these with a mallet, as they are used solely for paring and fine fitting; you are, however, allowed to use the palm of you hand to strike them and help things along. **Fig E** shows a similar chisel but this one is cranked so that it can be used at a very low angle. **Fig F** shows a chisel with a skewed bevelled edge which is designed to be used with a slicing action.

The swan-neck mortise chisel in **fig G** allows you to get deep into a mortise to chop and lever out any wood slivers or to flatten any irregularities, but its proper use is to work a curved bottom on the kind of mortise that is needed for shaped locks.

Fig H shows a drawer lock chisel and has the ends bent at right angles to the handle, one end being in the same plane as the handle and the other at right angles to it. It is used as shown in **fig 9** in places where an ordinary chisel is too large, such as on the back of a drawer front.

The Japanese have their own chisels, the Oire Nomi (shown in **fig 10**) and the similar but heavier Chu-uso. These have laminated blades in which the cutting edges are worked on specially hardened, high carbon steel sandwiched between tough, low carbon-steel laminations. Add to this the fact that they are hollow-ground on the back and you have a cutting edge which lasts much longer than those on conventional chisels.

GOUGES

These come in two types, as shown in **fig 11** opposite. The outside bevel, firmer gouge in **fig A**, also known as 'out-cannel', is used to cut and scoop out concave hollows or channels. The scribing, inside bevel, 'in-cannel' gouge in **fig B** is used for the upright cuts that will round off an edge.

9 **USING A DRAWER LOCK CHISEL**

HAMMER

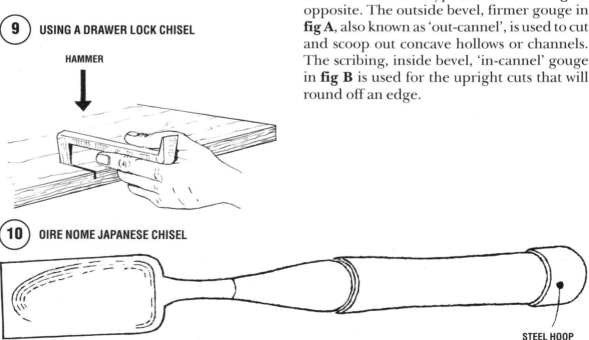

10 **OIRE NOME JAPANESE CHISEL**

STEEL HOOP

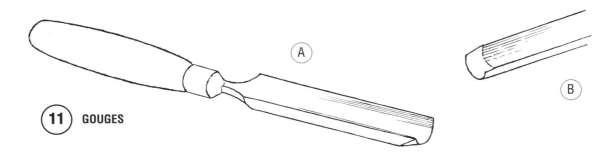

11 GOUGES

SPOKESHAVES

These tools, shown in **fig 12**, are essential if you are contemplating making reproductions of antique furniture, as there are few other tools capable of rounding off cabriole legs or claw feet – or in fact any job that involves working a smooth curve. There are two kinds: the wooden design shown in **fig A** and the metal one in **fig B**.

The wooden spokeshave can shape concave as well as convex curves. Also there are two separate metal designs, one having a flat face and the other a convex one, to cope with both kinds of curve. Both are usually pushed forward to cut with the grain, although there is no reason why you cannot pull them towards you if you wish.

One fault with the wooden design is that the tangs work loose in their holes, and the best way to cure this is to insert two screws as shown in **fig C** overleaf, filing off their points first.

12 SPOKESHAVES

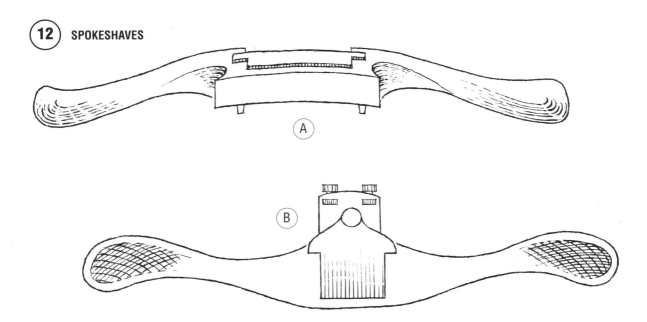

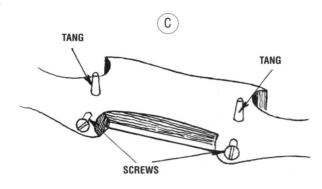

HAND PLANES

There are many kinds of hand plane and most have been rendered obsolete by power tools; this no doubt explains why they can be bought at auctions and car boot sales for next to nothing. The two which can still be useful in the workshop today are the bench plane and the block plane.

BENCH PLANE
Fig 13 opposite shows the parts of a typical bench plane. When the various components are adjusted properly, it is ideal for finishing small or narrow workpieces that would be difficult for a power plane. At the same time, it will plane a large area flat and true more quickly and effectively than its power counterpart.

The 250mm (10in) length is probably the handiest for normal work, but if you often have to deal with long workpieces, a jointer plane which can be 560mm (22in) long is capable of levelling lumps and hollows efficiently.

The main part of the plane is a casting, the bottom of which is called the sole, and this must be perfectly flat with the sides exactly at right angles so that the plane can be used on its side on a shooting board. These are points which must be checked when you buy, so it makes sense to take along a metal straightedge to

check the sole, and a try square to check the angles of the sides to the sole.

Although there is little you can do about faulty sides, you can true up the sole by removing the blade assembly and sliding the body backwards and forwards across an oilstone, or across a sheet of emery cloth taped totally flat and free of wrinkles on a piece of MDF. Sometimes you will find rough patches or small nibs on parts of the blade assembly or around the mouth, and these should be filed smooth so that everything fits snugly.

In operation, the cutting blade (also called the iron) and the back iron are butted together, and the amount by which the edge of the back iron stands back from that of the cutting blade determines the size of the shaving that is removed. For general work, it is about 1.5mm (1⁄16in) but you can move them closer together for a really fine cut.

The blade assembly sits on the frog and is held in place by a screw in the lever cap, which also has a spring lever cap to apply pressure. A screw at the back of the frog can be turned to adjust the size of the mouth, and a knurled wheel controls just how much of the blade protrudes and thus governs the depth of cut. A lateral adjustment lever allows you to move the setting of the blade sideways, which is particularly useful when replacing the blade after sharpening.

Note that, contrary to what you might expect, the bevel on the blade faces downwards and is ground by the manufacturer to an angle of 25 degrees; you then hone this on the oilstone and a strop to an angle of approximately 30 degrees. To finish off, dub off the sharp corners so that they do not cause ridges. There is a proper stance when planing which is not difficult to achieve: it involves starting the pass

(13) BENCH PLANE

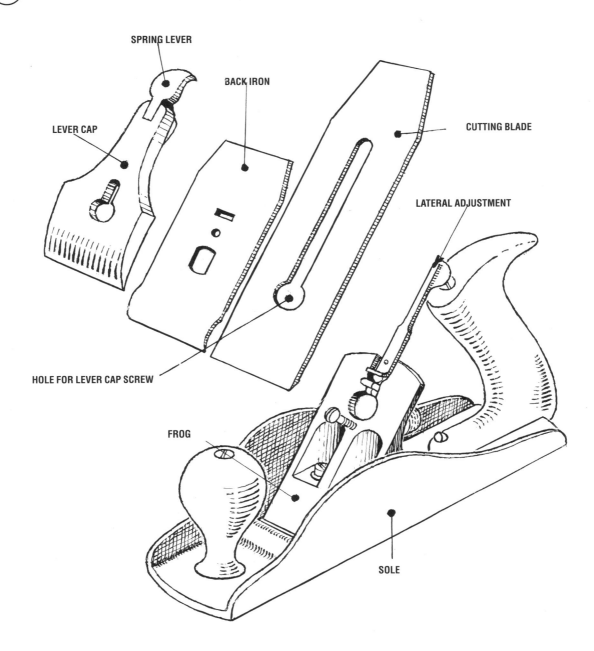

SPRING LEVER

BACK IRON

LEVER CAP

CUTTING BLADE

LATERAL ADJUSTMENT

HOLE FOR LEVER CAP SCREW

FROG

SOLE

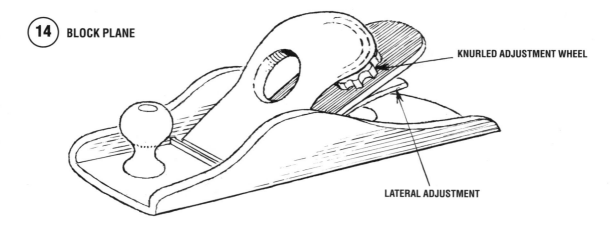

14 BLOCK PLANE

KNURLED ADJUSTMENT WHEEL

LATERAL ADJUSTMENT

by applying pressure at the front of the plane and transferring it to the back as you finish marking the cut.

You could buy a plane with replaceable throwaway blades – this would be an attractive alternative for anyone who does not use a plane very much and does not want the chore of blade sharpening. Some replacable blades can be re-sharpened but are so inexpensive that it seems hardly worth it. For the record, most of these planes have an attachment for rebating, but this is unlikely to interest the serious woodworker who prefers to work rebates with a router or on a sawbench.

Some manufacturers, mainly Continental ones, offer planes with wooden bodies and only the cutting assemblies in metal. These prob-ably appeal most to those who were brought up with wooden planes or who find a genuine delight in touching and handling wood.

BLOCK PLANE

The block plane, shown in **fig 14**, is invaluable for trimming small work and is worth having in any workshop. Unlike with the bench plane, the blade is fitted bevel uppermost so that there is only a tiny gap behind the cutting edge, and the angle at which the cutting blade is set is lower, at 20 degrees.

SMOOTHING PLANE IRON

This plane iron, shown in **fig 15**, is used for the final smoothing of wood, prior to glasspaper-ing ready for polishing. For a good finish, set the back iron as close as possible to the cutting edge as shown in **fig A**, and be careful to round off the corners of the latter very slightly as shown in **fig B**, to avoid digging in.

CABINET SCRAPER BLADE

Properly sharpened so that it removes fine shavings rather than dust, this can be used to finish off hardwood surfaces ready for polish-ing without further glasspapering. Although you can use it on softwood, it is sometimes too soft for the blade to grip properly. In fact, this is

15 SMOOTHING PLANE IRON

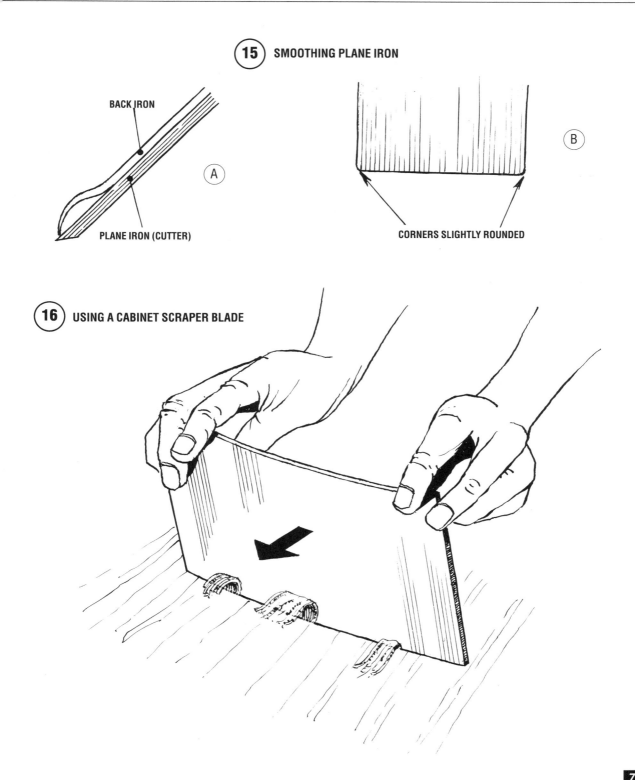

BACK IRON

PLANE IRON (CUTTER)

A

B

CORNERS SLIGHTLY ROUNDED

16 USING A CABINET SCRAPER BLADE

about the only tool that can deal with smoothing interlocked grain or difficult burr veneers.

Fig 16 on the previous page shows the correct way to use a scraper by inclining it forward at an angle and bending it slightly by pressing with the thumbs; how much effort is required depends on how well it has been sharpened. A handy size would be 100–150mm (4–6in) long by about 65mm (2½in) wide, and it should not be too thin or it will get uncomfortably hot in use – 2mm (⅟₁₆in) is about right.

HAND DRILLS

These are rapidly being replaced by power drills, especially the new battery-powered ones which are just as convenient as hand drills for making holes when no mains power is available as, for instance, when working in the garden. The double-pinion type shown in **fig 17** is better than the single-pinion as the action is smoother and easier.

17 HAND DRILL

WOOD-BORING BITS

Despite the proliferation of power tools, there are still many occasions when a brace or hand drill fitted with the appropriate bit can prove invaluable. A hand drill can be used in confined spaces and corners which a power tool could not reach, while a brace and bit, for example, can bore a 10mm (⅜in) diameter hole in 75mm (3in) thick timber with ease – and of course both are essential where there is no electricity.

Fig 18 shows the bits that are most popular today and their uses are explained below.

- **Centre bit (fig A)** Used to bore shallow holes or to bore right through thin wood, this bit is liable to wander if it is used for a deep hole. Note that the central point projects so that it can enter the wood and ensure that the hole is bored in exactly the right place. The nicker cuts the circumference and the cutter follows and lifts the waste which the nicker has loosened.

- **'Screw-point' centre bit (fig B)** This is similar to a centre bit but is so called as the screw thread pulls the bit into the wood. In common with the centre bit, it is fitted into a brace; when boring a hole with either bit, you should stop when the point just emerges from the underside, turn the wood over and complete the hole.

- **Forstner bit (fig C)** This bit is unique because it is guided by its rim (although there is a small point to enable you to start it) and it therefore produces a flat-bottomed hole. It can be used at any angle, to cut half a hole on the edge of a board or to make shallow sinkings for veneer and inlay work. Some woodturners use it in a lathe, although as it

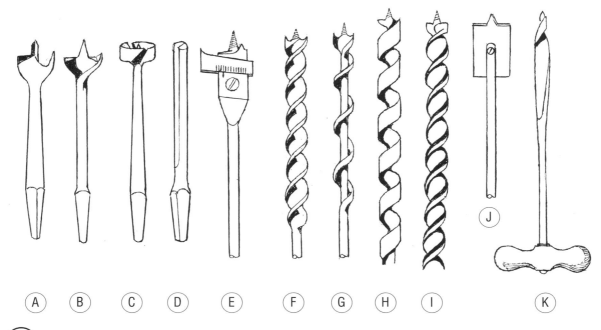

A   B   C   D   E   F   G   H   I   J   K

18 **WOOD-BORING BITS**

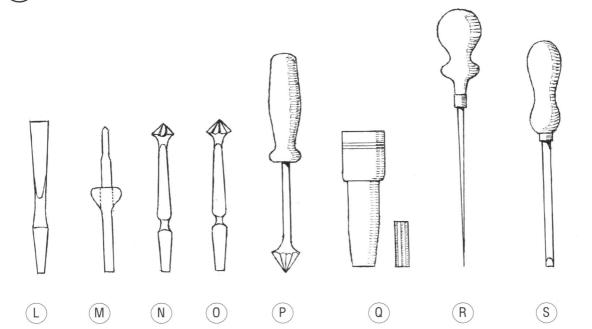

L   M   N   O   P   Q   R   S

is best for boring holes across the grain its partner, the sawtooth Forstner, which has saw teeth cut on its rim, is better as the teeth will enter end grain accurately and easily.

- **Shell bit (fig D)** This bit will start a hole very easily and is self-centring. It is popular with Windsor chair makers for boring the holes for the seats and for the sticks in the backs of Windsor chairs.

- **Expansive bits (fig E)** One of these will cut a range of sizes, as the diameter can be varied by aligning the scale on the cutter with a datum line on the body; it then behaves like a centre bit. There are two ranges of diameter available: 12–38mm (½–1½in) and 22–75mm (⅞–3in).

- **Jennings pattern twist bit (fig F)** This is so called because it was patented in 1855 by Russell Jennings – and any bit with such a long history must be good! This bit is particularly suitable for making deep holes, as the parallel helix brings the chips out as the bit enters and keeps the bit in alignment.

- **Irwin twist bit (fig G)** This is another bit with a long history and was patented by Charles Irwin in 1884. It comes into its own on heavy work, particularly in green wood, as the design ensures the waste is removed easily and quickly; the screw-thread tip pulls the bit into the wood with very little pressure.

- **Combination auger bit (fig H)** This bit can be used in either a traditional brace or a power drill on the slowest speed. The deep webs remove waste quickly and the wide lands ensure accuracy and a clean hole.

- **Scotch twist bit (fig I)** Used for rough work such as building sheds or fencing where a fine finish is not needed, this bit is speedy to use, with good waste removal.

- **Flat bit (fig J)** This recent design can be used with a hand drill to make shallow holes up to 38mm (1½in) in diameter. However, its main use is with a power drill for deep holes, and an extension shank 250mm (10in) long is available for this.

- **Half-twist bit (fig K)** Supplied with a handle to form a gimlet, this bit is very useful for making starter holes for small screws and is sometimes indispensable for use in very restricted spaces. The screw-thread tip pulls into the wood quickly and easily, and the large flute clears away waste efficiently.

- **Screwdriver bit (fig L)** This design is for use in a brace, when you can really apply leverage – easily as much as can be obtained using a power tool, although you do have to press down hard. If you have a ratchet brace, it is equally good at withdrawing stubborn screws. This bit can only be used on screws with slotted heads.

- **Counterbore bit (fig M)** This type of bit is made in various designs, but in all of them the end makes the hole for the screw threads and the next section forms the hole for the shank, while the shoulders shape the countersinking. It is best used in a power drill, but can also be employed with a hand drill.

- **Countersink bits: 'snail' (fig N) and 'rose' (fig O)** There is very little to choose between them. The snail is better used on a metal such as brass, while the rose is more appropriate for wood or plastics.

- **Hand countersink bit (fig P)** This bit will produce a shallow countersinking on thin or delicate wood, or it can be used to de-burr the edge of a hole.

- **Hand dowel-maker (fig Q)** This tool can be hammered into end grain to produce a dowel up to 38mm (1½in) long: it is the kind of tool furniture restorers use for making dowels from unusual or exotic woods where matching dowels are essential.

- **Joiner's awl or 'scratch' (fig R)** This tool has a 130mm (5in) long blade with a fine point and is used when very accurate marking out is required.

- **Bradawl (fig S)** This tool has a sharp edge, about 3mm (⅛in) wide at the end of its blade, and is used to make starter holes for screws or pins in thin materials.

ADHESIVES

The adhesives used in modern woodworking can be divided into three groups:

1 Adhesives which set by cooling, such as animal glues and 'hot melts'.
2 Adhesives which set by chemical reaction – a large group which includes UF (urea formaldehyde), PF (phenol formaldehyde), RF (resorcinol formaldehyde) and the epoxy resins.
3 Adhesives which set as a result of loss of moisture, the best known being PVA (polyvinyl acetate).

ANIMAL GLUES

The principal member of this group is the familiar Scotch glue, which is manufactured from the bones and hides of cattle. Used hot, it is particularly useful for veneering, as it can be re-melted easily by applying heat with a warm iron and a damp cloth. It has now been superseded in the workshop by the other adhesives mentioned above and the only woodworkers who are likely to use it are furniture restorers.

The most convenient kind to use is known as 'pearl' glue. The glue is heated before use in a pot suspended in hot water, which should not be allowed to boil. When it is ready for use it will run off the brush in a steady stream without any lumps and have the consistency of single cream.

Ideally the wood should be warmed, too, so that the glue is not chilled on contact. Apart from the ease with which it can be re-melted, other advantages of this glue are that it is as strong and durable in dry conditions as any of the other adhesives. It can be machined or cleaned off without blunting cutters, and it is almost non-staining, although the glue line may be noticeable when using light woods such as holly or sycamore.

Scotch glue is both cheap and relatively easy to use, and also its initial tackiness makes it invaluable for jobs such as putting in rubbed corner blocks. It has a long shelf life and a good pot life. However, it should not be re-heated too often or it will weaken. Its main disadvantage is that it has to be used quickly before it starts to cool, and therefore it may not be the best choice for a complicated job. It should never be used for outdoor work, because its resistance to moisture is virtually nil.

CHEMICAL REACTION

UF (urea formaldehyde) Nowadays, the big users of UF adhesives are plywood and particle-board makers, while furniture manufacturers use them for veneering, laminating and general assembly work. For home workshop use they are available in small packs in liquid or powder form. While the former may be more convenient to use as no pre-mixing is needed, it has a very short pot life. In powder form, the adhesive it will last up to two years or so without deterioration.

The adhesives comprise a resin and hardener. For woodworkers who have special needs, there is a large assortment of hardeners which will modify the characteristics of the adhesive to suit their requirements; most of us, however, will find little to complain about in the standard hardeners supplied in the packs.

These adhesives are reasonably capable of gap-filling and also resist damp, insect infestation and rot. In ordinary conditions, working time is about 10–20 minutes, but at least two hours cramping will be required before handling strength develops. Maximum strength will not be reached for several days – and not at all if the timber is cold and damp. Materials should therefore be stored in warm, dry conditions. One point to bear in mind is the risk of stains resulting from chemical reaction if any ferrous metal (such as steel) comes into contact with the adhesive before it has had time to set.

RF (resorcinol formaldehyde) These adhesives were developed to provide durability in tough outdoor conditions and boatbuilders in particular find them very useful. Structural engineers use them for laminated beams of the kind incorporated into modern buildings; in addition, they are perfectly capable of making durable bonds with certain non-wood materials such as brick, concrete, cork and leather. In normal use, the hardener and resin are pre-mixed and then spread on to both surfaces; unmixed, the shelf life is about 12 months.

Epoxy resins These provide the answers to many problems of adhesion. While some are specially tailored to meet precise requirements, there are general-purpose types available to the home woodworker which are suitable for fabricating strong load-bearing structures, though in practice their cost makes them expensive to use in quantity.

Because the bonding action is chemical, clean surfaces are required, but happily this also means that only the minimum quantity of the adhesive should be used for a joint – there should be no thick film, and there need be no wastage. There is no point in deliberately roughening the surfaces – light abrasion is quite enough – but cleanliness is essential. Glass and metals are among the impressive array of dissimilar materials that can be bonded satisfactorily with epoxies.

The adhesive comes in a pack containing two tubes – one for the resin and the other for the hardener – and they have an indefinite and very long shelf life provided resin and hardener do not come into contact.

You will need to apply suitable cramps and some form of heat while the joint is being made: cramping is usually relatively easy to arrange, and the latter requirement can often be met by placing the job in a domestic oven, on central-heating radiators or near some other convenient form of heating. Cold bonding without heat is possible, but it can be slow and may result in less than maximum strength.

3 LOSS OF MOISTURE

White PVA (polyvinyl acetate) Evostik Resin W is a popular example of this type of adhesive and is used by many woodworkers. In addition to using it undiluted, you can make up a solution of one part adhesive to four parts cold water and use it as a sealing agent for wood, brickwork or concrete. This can be applied to the end grain of wood before painting to prevent the fibres from soaking up the paint. If brushed thinly (or sprayed) on to an awkward piece of burr veneer which persists in cockling and left to dry under a weight (with a piece of waxed paper interposed) it will help to soften the grain and hold it flat.

The same solution stirred into a filler paste will improve its adhesive qualities and give a hard surface that can be sanded easily; it will, of course, make a coloured filler paler. Lastly, if the adhesive is mixed in the same proportion into the water used for making mortar, it will make good all those cracks and holes caused by moving heavy machinery or equipment about.

JIGS, TECHNIQUES AND TIPS FOR HAND WORK

1 BENCH HOOK

Strictly speaking, this device is not intended as a guide for the saw but to help you hold the work steady while sawing. The construction is simple: note that the edge piece is fastened to the base with dowels, because if screws were used there would always be the danger of the saw teeth hitting them.

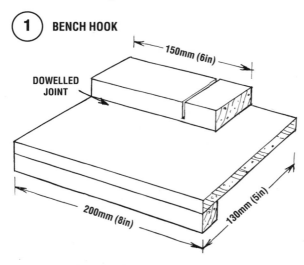

① BENCH HOOK

DOWELLED JOINT

150mm (6in)

200mm (8in)

130mm (5in)

2 SAWING DOWELS TO LENGTH I

When drilling holes for dowels, you can of course use a depth gauge to ensure that the dowels all protrude to the same length once they have been knocked in.

Another method, is to drill holes as near to the correct depth as you can judge and then knock in random lengths of dowel that are obviously too long. Holding a piece of scrap wood cut to the required depth against them enables you to saw them off to the correct length very quickly.

3 SAWING DOWELS TO LENGTH II

This jig consists of a block of straight-grained hardwood which has a strip screwed to its underside as shown, so that it can be held in the vice.

The three longitudinal holes need to be bored accurately, which means using either a lathe or a vertical drill stand fitted with a power drill and taken through the whole length.

Make a sawcut 25mm (1in) or so away from one end and then drill a series of transverse holes at regular intervals through the full width of the block. They must all be the same diameter so that a piece of dowel can be pushed through any of them to act as a stop.

4 PLANING HOLLOW SURFACES ON THIN BOARDS

These are notoriously difficult to deal with, but the device shown should solve the problem. It consists of a planing board which has a strip of wood with a bevel on its lower edge screwed along one side, depending on whether you are right- or left-handed. In use, one edge of the workpiece is caught under the bevel and the weight of the plane will then hold it flat.

(3) DOWEL SAWING JIG II

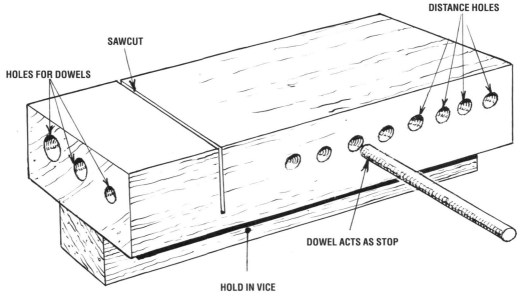

DISTANCE HOLES

SAWCUT

HOLES FOR DOWELS

DOWEL ACTS AS STOP

HOLD IN VICE

(4) JIG FOR PLANING HOLLOW SURFACES

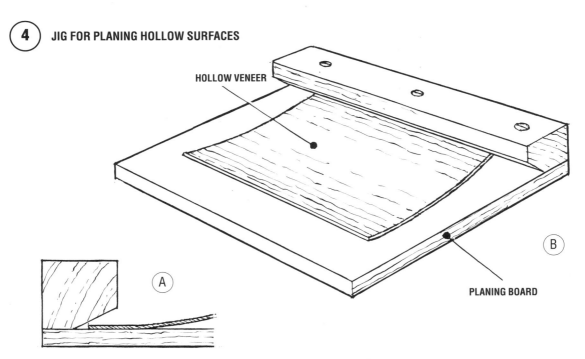

HOLLOW VENEER

(A)

(B)

PLANING BOARD

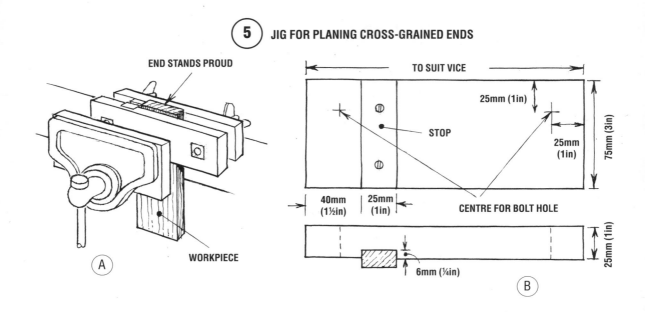

5 JIG FOR PLANING CROSS-GRAINED ENDS

5 PLANING CROSS-GRAINED ENDS

One of the most irksome jobs is trimming off the ends of rails without tearing out the wood, and this little device effectively guards against this happening.

Fig A shows how the jig is held in the vice with the end of the workpiece pushed tightly against the stops. These, combined with the fact that the end is allowed to protrude by the minimum amount to be planed off, should result in a perfect finish. **Fig B** shows an elevation and a plan of the jig. The dimensions given here are for guidance only, as it needs to be made to fit your particular vice.

6 IMPROVED BENCH STOP

If your bench is not fitted with a tail vice and bench dogs, try screwing one of these devices on the left side of your bench (or on the right side if you are left-handed). The stop is just a rectangular piece of 19mm (¾in) MDF with a notch cut out of it, into which a wedge is driven to hold the workpiece.

7 DRILLING JIG

This device will come in handy if you do not have a proprietary dowelling jig and have a job to do that involves making many dowelled-up frames for panels, such as those used for kitchen furniture. The jig does not take long to make and will help to ensure accurate joints.

As you can see in **fig A**, the device consists of a hardwood block (beech would be a good choice) which must be exactly the same thickness as the rail to be drilled, and its depth needs to be enough to guide the drill accurately – say 50mm (2in) as a minimum.

Drill the guide holes perfectly vertical in their exact locations and of a diameter to accept the dowels. The two cheeks should be screwed to the block sides, making sure that the screws do not interfere with the guide holes.

Fig B shows how the jig is cramped to a rail with the edges of the cheeks flush with its end.

6 IMPROVED BENCH STOP

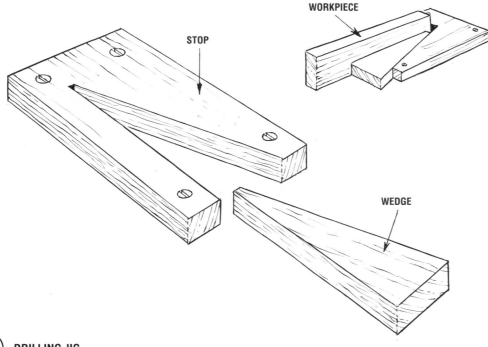

STOP

WORKPIECE

WEDGE

7 DRILLING JIG

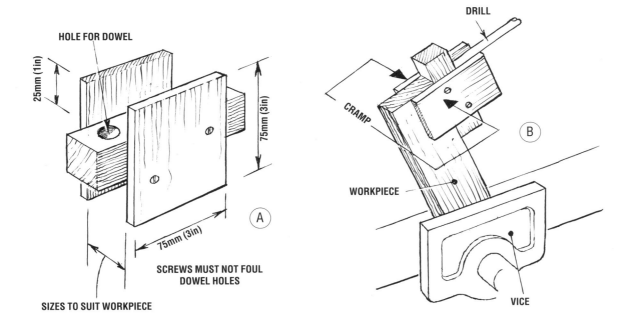

HOLE FOR DOWEL

25mm (1in)

75mm (3in)

75mm (3in)

A

SCREWS MUST NOT FOUL DOWEL HOLES

SIZES TO SUIT WORKPIECE

DRILL

CRAMP

B

WORKPIECE

VICE

8 CRADLE FOR HOLDING CYLINDERS

Holding a cylinder still while marking it out can be awkward, but this device enables you to mark out lines lengthwise and also at right angles to its length. Both these processes are often needed when working, for instance, on cylindrical chair or table legs.

The main component of the cradle is the vee block shown in **fig A**, which is made from two strips of wood with a 45 degree bevel worked on them, so that when they are glued together they form a cradle. A strong rubber band at each end should hold the cylinder in place and cutting off strips across an old car tyre inner tube will give you any number of suitable bands.

Fig B shows how the grasshopper gauge described on page 164 can be employed to slide along the cylinder edge and mark longitudinal lines: the stepped block can be slid along to mark off points at right angles to the length.

9 MITRE BLOCK

The figure gives details and dimensions for this block, which is suitable for sawing mitres on small mouldings. Although construction is straightforward, there are a couple of points to bear in mind.

First, it is worth letting the guide piece into a shallow rebate worked on the base, as this ensures that the pieces cannot be knocked off

8 CYLINDER CRADLE

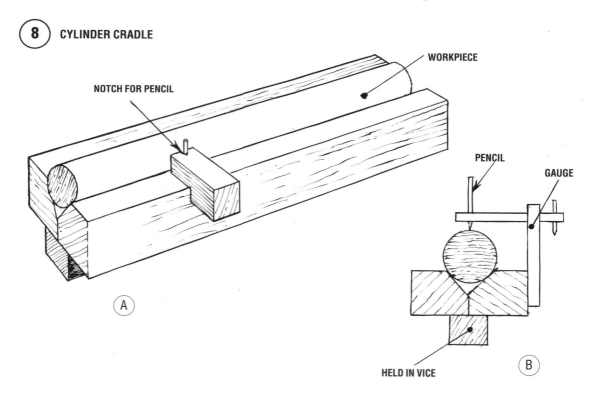

NOTCH FOR PENCIL

WORKPIECE

PENCIL

GAUGE

HELD IN VICE

A

B

accidentally. Second (as with the mitre box), a false base made of hardboard can be pinned lightly to the base to protect it from sawcuts, keeping the pins well away from the area where the saw will be used, of course.

10 MITRE BLOCK FOR REPEAT LENGTHS OF MOULDING

This gadget is particularly useful when you have a quantity of mouldings of the same length to mitre.

In **fig A**, **a** is a piece of timber to which another piece **b** of the same length is glued and screwed. Sectional **fig B** shows that the bottom edge of **b** stands up by about 19mm (¾in), so that it rests on the edge of the vice while the bottom part is gripped between the jaws. Piece **c** is a stop block which is held in place by a small cramp and is therefore adjustable, so that any length of moulding can be accommodated and mitred by means of the sawcuts **d** and **e**. If you so wish, you could also include a square cut as at **f**.

11 MITRE SHOOTING BOARD

This is an easily made solution to the problem of planing the ends of rails which have been mitred by sawing, to ensure that the angles are

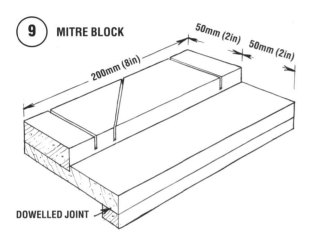

9 MITRE BLOCK

50mm (2in)
50mm (2in)
200mm (8in)

DOWELLED JOINT

10 MITRE BLOCK FOR MOULDING

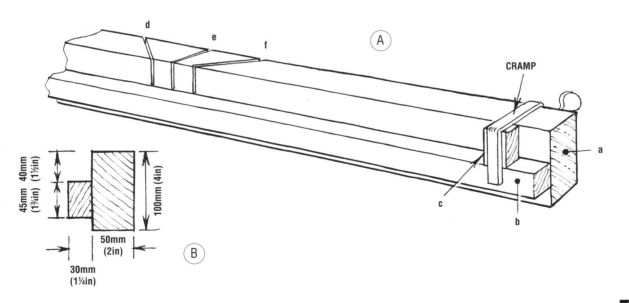

d
e
f
Ⓐ

CRAMP

45mm (1¾in)
40mm (1½in)
100mm (4in)
50mm (2in)
30mm (1¼in)
Ⓑ

a
c
b

MITRE SHOOTING BOARD

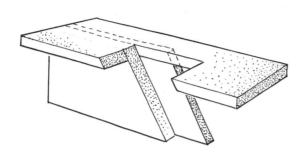

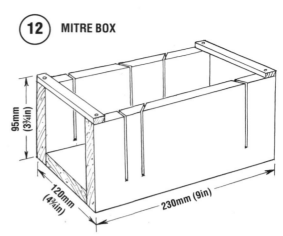
MITRE BOX

true, the faces smooth and the wood has not been torn out.

The figure shows the finished board, which could be made from MDF throughout, the parts being glued and screwed together. It can be held in the vice.

12 MITRE BOX

This is a useful design for a mitre box and the dimensions shown will give you a box which will accept quite large mouldings. Traditionally, these boxes were made from beech, but there is no reason why you should not use 15mm (⅝in) MDF instead.

The construction should be obvious from the figure, but what is not so clear is exactly how to cut the slots accurately. You could make up the box first and then cut them with a tenon saw, but this calls for a high degree of accuracy. A better way is to cut the slots on each piece before assembly and this could be done on the sawbench, utilizing one or other of the several jigs that are described in Chapter 3. As the saw is circular, the bottoms of the slots will be curved and therefore it will be necessary to cut the last portion by hand, but at least the partly cut slot will act as a guide.

The slots do not extend to the full depth by about 3mm (⅛in) and it is a good idea to fit a false bottom of hardboard which can be renewed from time to time.

13 JIG FOR STRENGTHENING MITRES

It is normal practice on smaller work such as trinket boxes, picture frames and the like which have mitred corners to strengthen them by 'keying', as shown in **fig A**.

The job involves making a couple of sawcuts into the mitre, as shown in **fig B**, into which small keys of veneer are glued, made of either matching or, sometimes, contrasting wood to produce a decorative finished appearance. Anything which makes the work easier, such as this jig, is very welcome.

To make the device as shown in **fig C**, a triangular former with an angle of exactly 90 degrees at the apex is glued and screwed to the backboard. A 6mm (¼in) coach bolt projects through a central hole sufficiently to accommodate the thickness of the workpiece and the clamp, the whole assembly being held together by a wing nut. A flat board is screwed and glued at right angles to the backboard along its upper edge, and this hooks over the

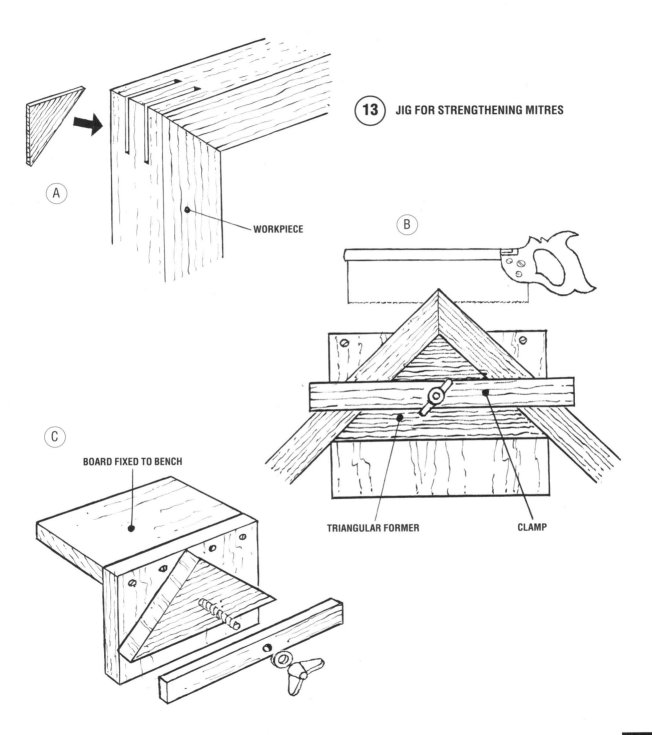

13 JIG FOR STRENGTHENING MITRES

(A)

WORKPIECE

(B)

(C)

BOARD FIXED TO BENCH

TRIANGULAR FORMER

CLAMP

edge of the bench and is held there by either screws or the bench holdfast. The veneer keys (properly called 'feathers') are made slightly oversize and trimmed off flush with a sharp chisel once the adhesive has set.

14 SUPPORT BLOCK FOR PLANING LONG PIECES

As you can see from the figure, this is a simple but effective gadget to support a long workpiece when it is held in the bench vice at one end, ready for planing. The block hooks over the edge of the bench, and the slotted piece must be the same thickness as the inner vice jaw. The cramp can be passed through the slot at any convenient height to hold the workpiece firmly in place.

Sizes are not significant and can be altered to use whatever offcuts you may have. If your bench is fitted with a tail vice, it would be a good idea to make the block wide enough to be held between the bench dogs.

15 EXTENSION TABLE FOR A VERTICAL DRILL STAND

You may have found that workpieces are frequently too large to rest conveniently on the bed of your drill stand – this extension table solves the problem. It comprises two halves which are jigsawn to butt together. They can be held together with a hook and eye when in use, and if holes are drilled in them they can hang on the wall when not in use.

16 FOLDING WEDGES

These are identically shaped wedges which, although they appear primitive, can prove indispensable in the most 'hi-tech' workshop.

Fig A shows how to make a pair, and the dimensions given here will result in two useful general-purpose wedges with a slope of about 15 degrees. This gives good results, although you may have to make some to a special size for a particular job.

In **fig B**, the wedges are employed as very

14 SUPPORT BLOCK FOR PLANING LONG PIECES

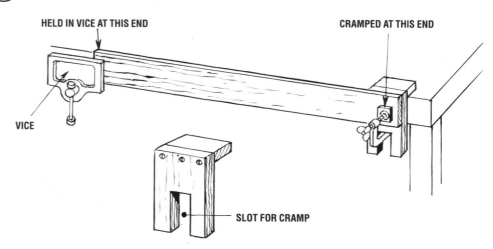

HELD IN VICE AT THIS END

CRAMPED AT THIS END

VICE

SLOT FOR CRAMP

(15) EXTENSION TABLE FOR A VERTICAL DRILL STAND

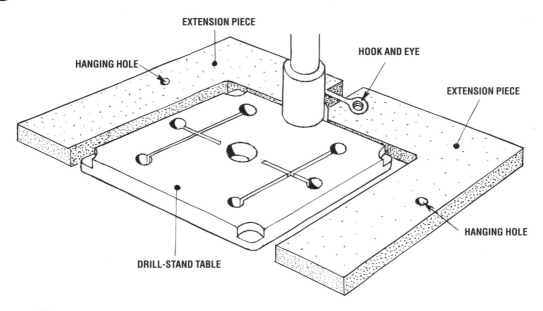

HANGING HOLE

EXTENSION PIECE

HOOK AND EYE

EXTENSION PIECE

HANGING HOLE

DRILL-STAND TABLE

(16) FOLDING WEDGES

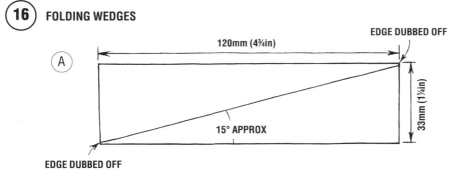

(A)

120mm (4¾in)

EDGE DUBBED OFF

33mm (1¼in)

15° APPROX

EDGE DUBBED OFF

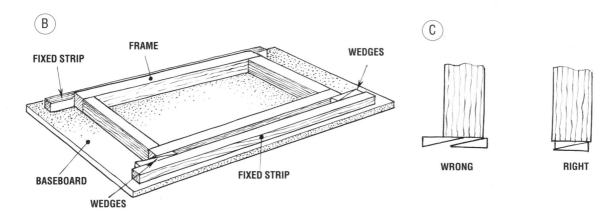

(B)

FIXED STRIP

FRAME

WEDGES

BASEBOARD

WEDGES

FIXED STRIP

(C)

WRONG

RIGHT

effective cramps on a job which is too large for normal cramps and they can exert a surprising amount of pressure.

This fact leads on to **fig C**, which shows how the wedges can be used for tightening posts in circumstances where they have to be cut short deliberately so that they can be introduced into an existing frame. The important point to note is that the posts must rest on the thickness of *both* wedges: if not, the tapered ends can easily be crushed and the wedging effect lost.

17 SASH CRAMP USED FOR HOLDING WIDE BOARDS

The arrangement shown in plan in the figure is useful for holding a wide board while planing it, and consists of a sash cramp gripped in the bench vice to hold the board steady.

Vices vary in pattern and you will almost certainly have to insert packing blocks on each side of the cramp bar to make room for the cramp heads and so you can turn the cramp handle.

18 HOLDING LARGE BOARDS FOR EDGE PLANING

Most man-made boards are heavy, and man-handling one measuring 2440 x 1220mm (8 x 4ft) while working on it can be exhausting. With the possible help of a partner, the small feet shown in **figs A** and **B** will hold a board upright while you work on planing it lengthwise.

Each foot is simply a short length of stout timber: a typical size could be 100 x 75 x 305mm (4 x 3 x 12in). At the central point, cut a trench wide enough to accept the thickest board you are likely to use – which will normally be 19mm (¾in) – plus an allowance for fitting it; this means that the final width should be about 25mm (1in).

Finally, work a tapered notch on one side of the trench so that it forms a step into which you can drive a suitably shaped wedge. Three of these feet should be sufficient to hold a 2440mm (8ft) board upright, ready for planing.

(17) SASH CRAMP SET-UP FOR HOLDING WIDE BOARDS

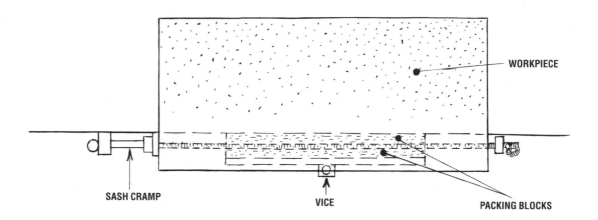

WORKPIECE

SASH CRAMP

VICE

PACKING BLOCKS

18 FEET TO HOLD LARGE BOARDS FOR EDGE PLANING

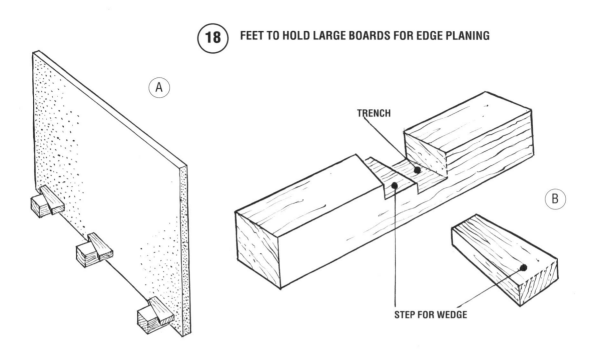

TRENCH

A

B

STEP FOR WEDGE

19 STICKING BOARD

This device is so called because it is a planing board with a small spike (usually a clipped-off nail) protruding in such a way as to hold the workpiece steady.

The design shown here is an improvement on this basic idea because as well as a spike, a sliding block is used to hold the workpiece. A slot is cut in the planing board and a sliding block runs along it, which can be tightened at any point by means of a wing nut threaded on to a dowel screw. The board is particularly handy because it can be constructed to accommodate contemporary power planes which, of course, need quite a lot more space than hand planes.

19

STICKING BOARD

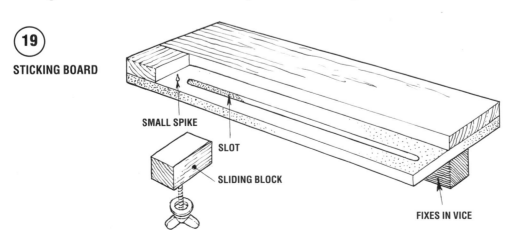

SMALL SPIKE

SLOT

SLIDING BLOCK

FIXES IN VICE

20 HOLDING SHAPED WORKPIECES IN THE VICE

It sometimes happens that a workpiece with a slight shaping and few, if any, straight edges – such as an oval – has to be held in the vice jaws, but these cannot get enough purchase to prevent it from tilting.

20 **SET-UP FOR HOLDING SHAPED WORKPIECES**

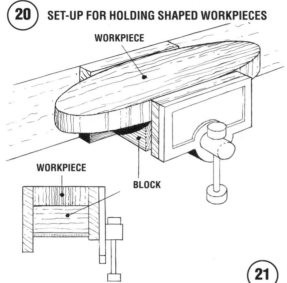

WORKPIECE

WORKPIECE

BLOCK

To overcome this problem, fix the workpiece temporarily on a block of scrap wood of the requisite thickness with double-sided adhesive tape, which in turn can rest on the vice guides as shown and prevent the work from tilting.

21 HOLDING CHAIRS IN THE VICE

This is the set-up used by trade chair makers for cleaning up chair and stool frames, and by cabinet makers working when they are on small tables or cabinet frames.

The figure shows the arrangement: the frame being worked on has two of its legs on the bench top and the other two inserted under it, while a convenient length of scrap wood and the vice are used to cramp it in place. If your bench has an apron piece, G-cramps could be employed instead of the vice.

21 **SET-UP FOR HOLDING CHAIRS**

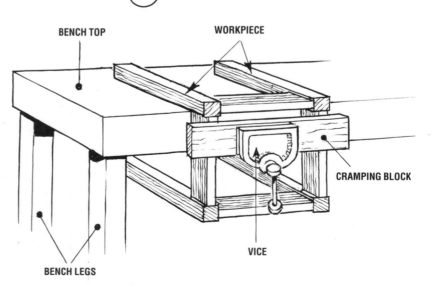

BENCH TOP

WORKPIECE

CRAMPING BLOCK

VICE

BENCH LEGS

22 WORKMATE ROLLER STAND

It is easy to make one of these by building a frame with a roller mounted on the top, which can be cramped between the Workmate jaws at various heights. Although it works effectively, it suffers from the disadvantage that you can only easily move the workpiece backwards or forwards: it is difficult to move it sideways.

The design shown overcomes this problem by utilizing a set of twin-wheel castors which have screw-on plate fixings, which are very free running and swivel readily. Alternatively, you can use special universal transfer balls (recently introduced by the Axminster Power Tool Centre – see Suppliers), as they are pur- pose-built and can be mounted with ordinary bolts. In addition, the vertical edges on one side of the frame are notched to fit over one of the jaws at levels that enable the working height to be adjusted to coincide with the height of your saw table, bandsaw or bench. Clearly the frame needs to be robust, and the timber you

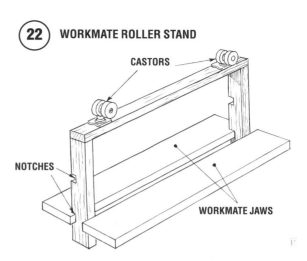

22 WORKMATE ROLLER STAND

CASTORS

NOTCHES

WORKMATE JAWS

make it from should be about 75 x 38mm (3 x 1½in) with cross rails at top and bottom.

23 WORKMATE CRAMPING JIG

These benches are already well known for their versatility and this device means you can cramp up a larger workpiece – a useful facility in these days of large man-made boards.

The jig comprises four arms that can be

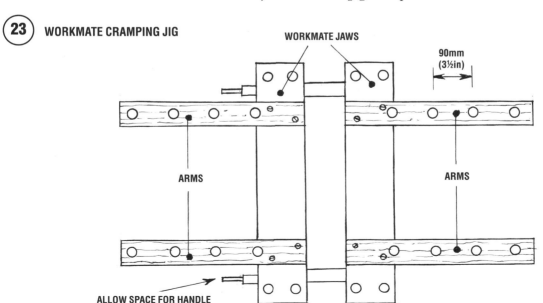

23 WORKMATE CRAMPING JIG

WORKMATE JAWS

90mm
(3½in)

ARMS

ARMS

ALLOW SPACE FOR HANDLE

bolted to the Workmate by means of counter-sunk-head bolts plus wing nuts inserted through holes bored in the jaws. As the jaws open up to 100mm (4in), if you bore holes in the arms every 90mm (3½in) or so in order to accept the dogs supplied with the Workmate, you should be able to accommodate a wide range of workpiece sizes.

24 EDGE-JOINTING BOARDS

Most panels used in furniture these days consist of man-made boards, but many wood-workers have pieces of natural timber (often from old furniture that has been broken up) which if they could be assembled edge to edge would make, say, an attractive occasional table.

The usual methods of joining such pieces are to fix them together with either a biscuit jointer, a loose tongue or dowels. However, there are two other ways of doing the job that are well worth knowing: rub-jointing and slot-screwing.

Rub-jointing This is also called 'slape' jointing. The principle involved is that an adhesive is applied to the meeting edges, which are then rubbed against each other lengthwise as shown in **fig A**; this expels most of the adhesive but, with the suction created, enough is left to hold the pieces together firmly. Until the arrival of plywood and other man-made boards this was one of the recognized ways to do the job, and the fact that many pieces of antique furniture on which the method was employed still survive proves its efficacy. Scotch glue was the only one available in the old days and can still be used, in addition to most modern synthetic resin adhesives except casein.

The end grain of adjoining boards must be opposed as shown in **fig B**, so that any tendency

to cup or warp is minimized. The edges must be perfectly flush and square – if you have an overhand plane or a power plane this should not be a problem. Using a hand plane can be more difficult, and the most effective method in all cases is to hold the boards side by side in a vice or with G-cramps and plane the edges together. The best way of testing the boards for truth is to place them on top of one another as shown in **fig C** and swivel them against each other, when you will be able to locate any high spots that require smoothing away.

Fig D shows how to glue both edges simultaneously, which is to be recommended strongly if you are using Scotch glue as the work has to be done quickly to avoid it chilling – it also helps if the pieces can be warmed before

RUB-JOINTING

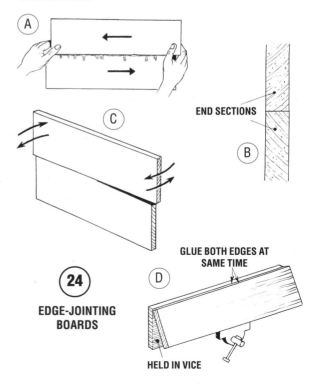

END SECTIONS

GLUE BOTH EDGES AT SAME TIME

(24)
**EDGE-JOINTING
BOARDS**

HELD IN VICE

starting by placing them near a source of heat such as a central-heating radiator. The pieces are then slid backwards and forwards as shown in **fig A** for 50–75mm (2–3in), until all air is expelled and the face marks coincide, when they can be stacked.

This procedure is sufficient for joints up to 1m (39in) long left uncramped: longer joints should be cramped with sash cramps about 300mm (1ft) apart.

Slot-screwed joint In this joint, a countersunk-head screw is driven into the edge of one board

and its head left projecting for about 13–15mm (½–⅝in), while a hole is bored with a slot alongside it in the edge of the other board. The arrangement is shown in **fig A**, and the dimensions of the screw hole and the slot are given in **fig B**.

The screws here should be inclined very slightly in the direction the boards are to be driven, as shown in **fig C** below, so that their heads cut into the slots and hold the boards firmly together. The edges of the boards are, of course, given a coat of adhesive before this is done.

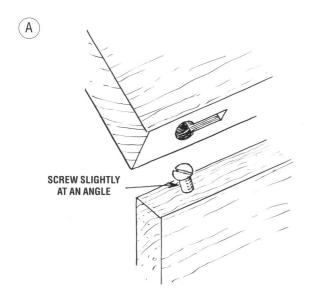

A

SCREW SLIGHTLY
AT AN ANGLE

SLOT-SCREWED JOINT

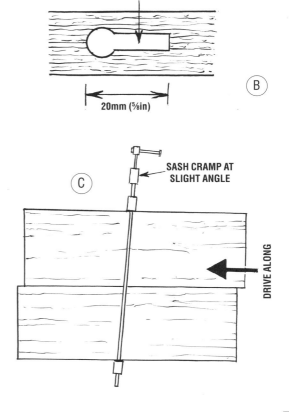

WIDTH SLIGHTLY LARGER
THAN SCREW SHANK

20mm (⅝in)

B

C

SASH CRAMP AT
SLIGHT ANGLE

DRIVE ALONG

25 EASIER JOINT SAWING

This tip is handy when cutting shoulders for tenons or halved joints by hand.

Mark the lines for the joint with a pencil and try square in the usual manner and then score a line across the piece with a craft knife held vertically, making it as deep as you can. Then make another cut at 45 degrees alongside the first and the result will be a notched groove into which you can put the saw teeth – it will also give a cleaner finish to the joint.

26 BRIDGE CRAMPING

The technique shown in the figure is particularly useful in furniture restoration, for instance when a highly polished or veneered surface needs to be cramped down and G-cramps would mark the surface even if protective pads were used (as they always should

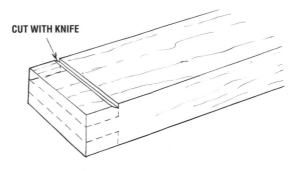

CUT WITH KNIFE

be, of course). It is also an extremely handy technique for cramping down awkward pieces which do not provide a great deal of purchase for the cramps. Note that the block on which the bridge rests at one end must be exactly the same thickness as the workpiece.

26 **BRIDGE CRAMPING**

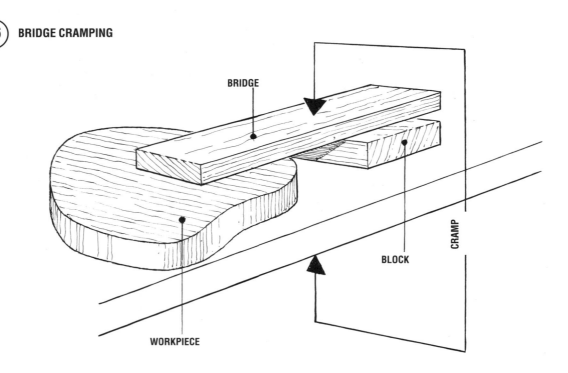

BRIDGE

CRAMP

BLOCK

WORKPIECE

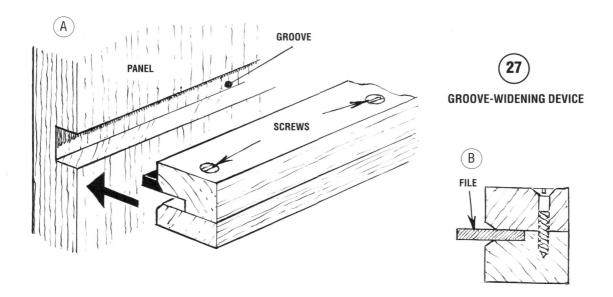

27 WIDENING A GROOVE

The gadget shown in **figs A** and **B** will help if you have to fit a polished or veneered shelf into a groove which is too tight. Obviously, you need either to plane a shaving off the shelf – which will almost certainly damage the polish or veneer – or widen the groove slightly.

To make the device, a flat file is held between two strips of wood about 60mm (2⅜in) longer than itself, one of the strips being rebated by an amount slightly less than the thickness of the file; the innermost corners of both strips are dubbed off to provide clearance for the dust. The file is held between the strips by means of a screw at each end, so that it can be adjusted to protect the depth of the groove. It can then be worked backwards and forwards until the groove has been widened sufficiently.

28 PELLETS AND PLUGS

Now that modern furniture is frequently made from pine, knots have become acceptable and are often considered to enhance its appearance. Unfortunately there is always the risk that a small one will fall out and spoil an otherwise attractive piece; however, there are ways of dealing with the problem.

One is to turn up a few pellets from a matching offcut, bore a hole to cover the area left by the offending knot and then glue in one of the pellets. Don't be tempted to use a short piece of dowel instead as the end grain will necessarily be exposed and will absorb far more stain and polish than the surrounding wood, thereafter standing out like the proverbial sore thumb. As shown in **fig A**, the direction of grain in a pellet allows you to match it with the surrounding wood, and if there should be any future shrinkage it will be to the same degree as the remainder of the wood.

However, turning pellets on the lathe can be a tricky business as they are so small. A good alternative is to invest in a few plug cutters of various sizes. **Fig B** shows a typical design which can be inserted in a power drill to produce a number of plugs quickly, all with the grain running in the required direction.

29 ATTACHING A TABLE TOP TO A FRAME

The figure shows five traditional methods of attaching table tops to frames.

Fig A shows a glue block. This needs to be pressed down and rubbed backwards and forwards to expel any air; because only animal glue is suitable for this method, it is very rarely used today.

In **fig B** a gouge is used to form a pocket and a screw is driven through at the end. No adhesive should be used, which means that the top can be removed if necessary.

Fig C shows a similar method, but this time the pocket is cut with a chisel.

Fig D shows one of the best methods. A turn-button is screwed to the underside of the top and has a tongue which fits tightly into a slot cut in the frame rail. The fixing should not be too tight, however, as the aim is that the top and frame rail should be able to shrink or swell independently.

Fig E shows the well-known metal shrinkage plate. The flange with the slots is screwed to the underside of the top with round-head screws, which should not be driven home too tightly, and the other flange is screwed to the frame rail with countersunk-head screws in the usual way.

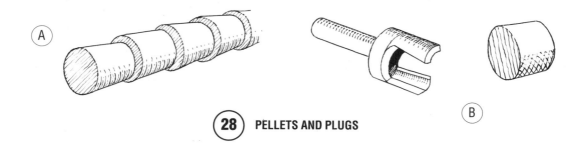

(A)

28 PELLETS AND PLUGS

(B)

(29) **ATTACHING A TABLE TOP TO A FRAME**

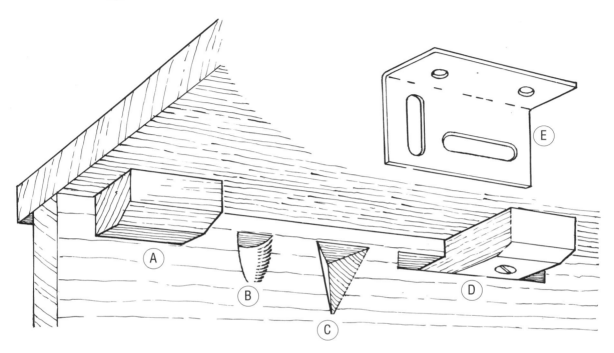

30 TIPS FOR USING NAILS

Before starting to nail, make sure that the face of the hammer is free from old paint or any form of grease or oil, otherwise it may glance off the head of the nail and bend it as it is being driven in. All you need to do is occasionally rub the face on a piece of glasspaper.

When nailing together two pieces of wood of different thicknesses, whenever possible nail the thin one to the thick in order to get the best grip.

Always use the correct size of nail for the job – there is a wide choice available. If you have to pre-drill a hole, remember that it must not be so large that the nail slides in almost without being hammered.

Nailing close to the edge or the end of a workpiece will almost certainly result in the

(30) **NAILING METHODS**

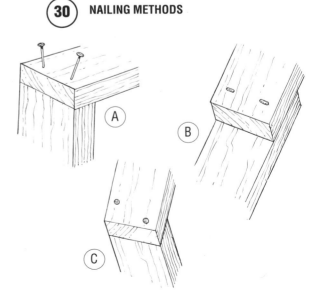

wood splitting where the fibres have been forced apart. Tapping the tip of a nail with a hammer will create a blunt point which is less likely to split the wood; however, try to avoid having to nail in such circumstances.

The figure on the previous page shows three ways of using nails. In **fig A,** each is driven inwards at an angle – this is called 'dovetail nailing' and results in a strong fixing. The two pieces of wood in **fig B** have grain running in the same direcion, and driving in oval-headed nails with their heads aligned across the grain will reduce the risk of splitting. **Fig C** shows how staggering the nails when driving them into end grain will also greatly help to prevent splitting.

(31) EXTRACTING NAILS

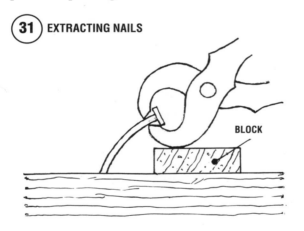

BLOCK

31 EXTRACTING NAILS

You will find this job is made easier if you place a small block of wood under the pincers or the head of a claw hammer, as shown. Not only does this prevent bruising, it also provides greater leverage.

32 COLLECTING SPILT NAILS

The answer to this is, of course, to use a magnet – but how can you then prise off a hundred or so veneer pins that are determined to hold on? Try holding a handkerchief or a piece of paper over the ends of the magnet, which will still function perfectly, and then hold everything over the container and gently take the magnet away.

33 THE HUMBLE CANDLE END

Old-time cabinet makers rubbed a candle end on screw threads to ease the labour of inserting screws: not only was this most effective, but it also made the job of withdrawing the screws at a later date much easier.

A quick rub of a candle end along saw teeth makes sawing smoother, especially in hardwoods, and it has the same effect on the soles of wooden planes. It is also well known that rubbing a candle along drawer runners ensures that the drawers will run sweetly.

Chapter 6

SHARPENING DEVICES AND TECHNIQUES

lthough sharpening saws yourself can be a difficult and time-consuming job, it is still a skill worth mastering provided the saws are of good quality. This chapter presents a range of techniques, tips and devices to help you with this and other, more straightforward sharpening tasks in the home workshop. It also explains how to use the various different sharpening stones available today, and provides a neat design for a box and blade holder to prevent wear on the oilstone.

HAND SAWS

Before re-sharpening a hand saw there are several points to consider, as the work is time-consuming, requires a great deal of patience and you can easily ruin a saw in the process. For saws with smaller teeth, such as panel saws and backsaws, good eyesight is essential – I use a magnifying glass mounted on a stand and a desk lamp for good lighting as well.

If you do not feel up to doing the job yourself you can send your saws away for sharpening, but then there is the cost to consider as well as the chore of packing them. It may be worthwhile investing in hardpoint saws

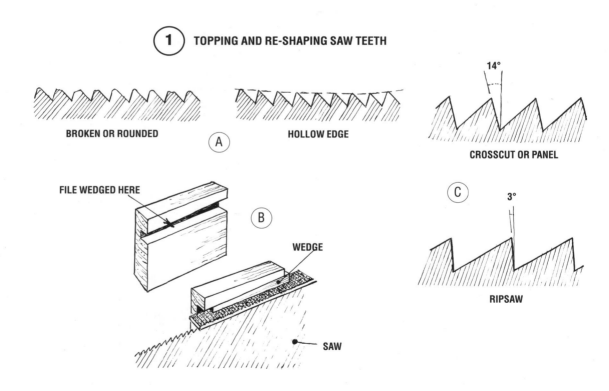

1 TOPPING AND RE-SHAPING SAW TEETH

BROKEN OR ROUNDED   HOLLOW EDGE   Ⓐ

FILE WEDGED HERE   Ⓑ   WEDGE   SAW

14°   CROSSCUT OR PANEL   Ⓒ   3°   RIPSAW

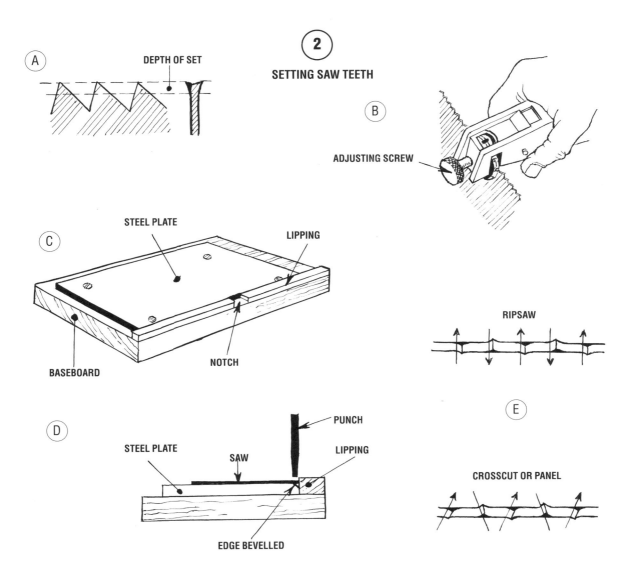

A — DEPTH OF SET

2
SETTING SAW TEETH

B — ADJUSTING SCREW

C — STEEL PLATE — LIPPING — NOTCH — BASEBOARD

RIPSAW

D — STEEL PLATE — SAW — PUNCH — LIPPING — EDGE BEVELLED

E

CROSSCUT OR PANEL

(which cannot be sharpened – see page 67) and then buying replacements when you have to throw them away.

Holding the saw securely while sharpening it is obviously essential and a suitable jig is described on page 110.

The process of topping as shown in **fig 1**

consists of making sure that the points of the teeth are not chipped or broken and that they are all in a straight line, as shown in **fig A**. The job is done with a flat file held in the gadget shown in **fig B**, which ensures that the file is presented squarely. It should only be done lightly and in several passes if necessary.

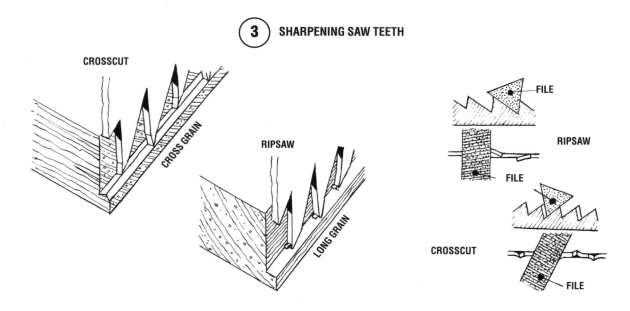

3 SHARPENING SAW TEETH

When re-shaping the teeth, which is the next step, they should protrude only about 6mm (¼in) beyond the jaws so that they are well supported. Use a triangular file with faces that are at least twice the depth of the teeth, and stroke it exactly at right angles to the blade and perfectly horizontally. Usually the file will settle into the gullet at the existing angle of pitch, but if not, the correct angles are 3 degrees for ripsaws and 14 degrees for crosscut, as shown in **fig 3**.

Fig 2 on the previous page shows the major factors to watch when setting the teeth. **Fig A** shows that only the outer part (slightly less than half) is in fact bent over to form the 'set', otherwise the tooth could break off at the root and spoil the cutting ability of the saw. There are two ways you can apply the set: by means of saw-setting pliers as shown in **fig B**, or by using the home-made device shown in **fig C**.

The pliers are better for the amateur to use, because you simply turn an anvil until the number of teeth per 25mm (1in) you require

appears and then, by simply squeezing the handle, a plunger (the hammer) pushes the tooth over.

The device shown in **fig C** is made by mounting a piece of steel plate on to a wooden baseboard. A piece of steel about 10mm (⅜in) thick would be suitable, and it can be held in place either by a beading fixed around three edges or by screwing to the baseboard, so that a wooden lipping can be pinned along the front of one of the longer edges of the plate, which has its edge bevelled off at 45 degrees. The lipping has a small notch cut in the centre, so that when the saw teeth are butted against it only one tooth is exposed. The method of setting, as shown in **fig D**, is to place a nail punch (with its end filed off square) on it and hit the punch lightly with a hammer to bend the tooth over. A 75mm (3in) nail with the point sawn off square also makes a good punch. The punch is applied to alternate teeth on one side of the saw blade and then the blade is turned over so that the remaining teeth can be set.

Now for the last stage – the sharpening. As shown in **fig 3** opposite, the different jobs that ripsaws, panel saws and crosscut saws have to do means that while the teeth on a ripsaw are filed at 90 degrees to the saw blade, those on the other two types of saw are filed at about 50 degrees. Strictly speaking, if a crosscut saw is to be used to cut hardwood, the angle should be 60–65 degrees and on softwood 45 degrees, so the 50 degrees is a compromise which can include panel saws.

Try to do the sharpening with one light pass of the file, otherwise the tooth shape will become distorted. As with the setting, alternate teeth are sharpened on one side first and then the saw is turned over for the other teeth to be dealt with.

It is quite difficult to maintain a consistent angle with the file. If you are using the jig described on page 110, you can mark the angle by pencilling on the white plastic edge and using this as a guide; otherwise, you can pencil some lines on the bench. It is also important to know how far you have reached in case you have to break off work in the middle of the process. To do this, some woodworkers give the points of the teeth a light stroke of the file before they start, which makes the points shine; as they are sharpened, the shine disappears. I rub a piece of blackboard chalk along them, and this also disappears as the teeth are sharpened.

BACKSAWS

The techniques for shaping, setting and sharpening hand saws also apply to backsaws, except that dovetail and gent's saws have no set on the teeth. The prospect of dealing with a 22 or 24 TPI (teeth per inch) backsaw is a pretty daunting one, and unless you have had previous experience is not one to be encouraged – this is where hardpoint-toothed saws begin to look very attractive! If there is no escape and you have another blade which has the same number of teeth (and hacksaws sometimes do), you could clamp the two side by side so that you have something to guide you.

Fig 4 shows how to tighten a loose blade on a backsaw by resting the saw on a wooden block and tapping the back down with a hammer.

4 **TIGHTENING A LOOSE BACKSAW BLADE**

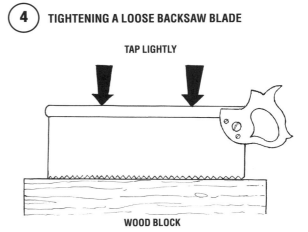

TAP LIGHTLY

WOOD BLOCK

CIRCULAR SAWS

The majority of these are TCT (tungsten-carbide-tipped) and cannot be sharpened; even with high-speed steel saws, it is best to restrict treatment to just a light sharpening, as it could be hazardous to set the teeth yourself.

SAW SHARPENING JIG

The jig shown in **fig 5** will prove to be a great asset if you are contemplating sharpening and setting your own saws. It is sawn from a white plastic-faced board such as Contiboard that has plastic-covered edges on which you can make

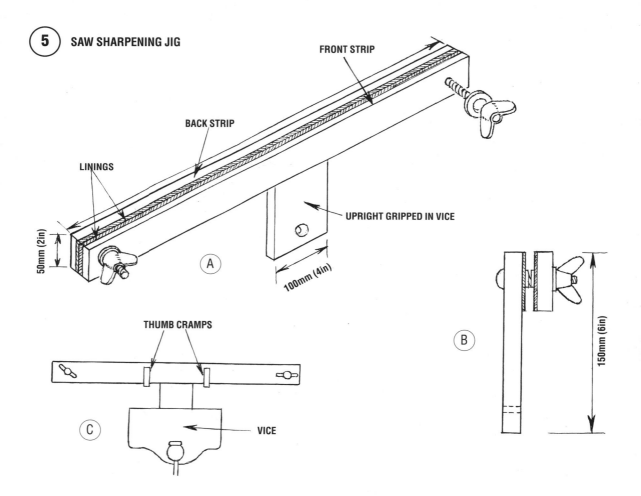

5 SAW SHARPENING JIG

FRONT STRIP

BACK STRIP

LININGS

50mm (2in)

UPRIGHT GRIPPED IN VICE

100mm (4in)

A

THUMB CRAMPS

B

150mm (6in)

C

VICE

a pencil mark to indicate how far you have reached, in case you have to stop work unexpectedly. This is more of an advantage than it might appear at first sight, as resuming sharpening without this knowledge can mean filing several teeth twice and this can spoil the level of the teeth along the blade.

Figs A and **B** show how the jig is assembled. The back strip is sawn in the shape of a T with a short upright piece, and only the lower part of this is gripped in the vice. The front piece is the same, except that it is a straight strip without the upright, and the length of both strips is governed by the length of the longest saw you will be sharpening.

A hole is drilled about 25mm (1in) from each end of the pieces, and bolts, wing nuts and washers are inserted through these so that the strips can be pulled together. In addition, each bolt carries a spring washer which fits between the strips and acts as a spacer. It is a good idea to glue linings of leather or felt on the inside faces to absorb vibration and prevent the screeching noise that will otherwise accompany filing the teeth.

Fig C shows the assembly set up for use. The saw blade fits in between the strips and the bolts and wing nuts hold it firmly in place – it does mean that the saw must be removed, but this is a simple matter of unscrewing three shallow nuts and bolts. Two thumb cramps are positioned as shown to equalize the pressure along the whole length of the saw.

Finally, a hole can be drilled in the upright for hanging the jig on a wall when not in use.

CHISELS

Manufacturers supply chisels with the edges already ground to an angle of 25 degrees and it is up to the woodworker to hone the edge to about 30 degrees on the oilstone. Experienced workers can judge this by eye and can carry out the work without any aid to guide them, but a honing guide as shown in **fig 6** is a great help and will enable you to maintain the same bevel every time. Equally important is the need to lap the back of the chisel by holding it perfectly flat on the stone and rubbing it in a circular motion until you get a mirror finish, so that the cutting edge is where two highly polished surfaces meet.

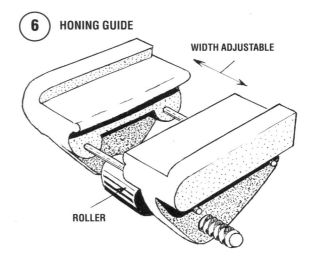

6 HONING GUIDE

WIDTH ADJUSTABLE

ROLLER

Sharpening on the oilstone will create a burr or 'wire edge' on the edge and you can both see and feel it. Remove it by stropping the blade on a strop made from a piece of leather glued to a block of wood. Dress the leather with a paste of emery powder and a light machine oil: I use the finest grade of cutting-back paste as used by car body sprayers, which is sold by car accessory shops. Japanese chisels are best sharpened on a Japanese water stone or one of the new diamond stones.

Finally, if you need a chisel to go into awkward places such as chopping out a dovetail socket as shown in **fig 7**, a useful tip is to grind off the corners. If done in moderation, this will not weaken the chisel.

7 CHISEL FOR AWKWARD PLACES

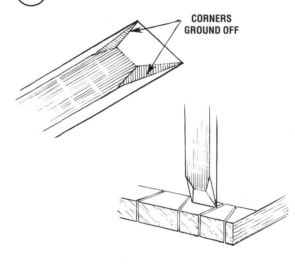

CORNERS GROUND OFF

8 SHARPENING A FIRMER GOUGE

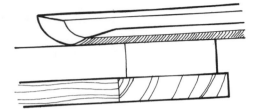

9 SHARPENING A SCRIBING GOUGE

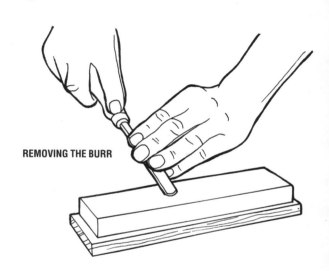

REMOVING THE BURR

GOUGES

The out-cannel or firmer gouge is sharpened using a rocking movement on the stone, as shown in **fig 8**. This will, of course, create a burr on the inside, which must be removed with an oilstone slip of the right curvature.

The in-cannel bevel on a scribing gouge is also sharpened with an oilstone slip; in **fig 9** the resulting burr is removed by rocking the tool.

CABINET SCRAPERS

Fig 10 shows the various stages in sharpening a cabinet scraper. **Fig A** shows an enlarged section of the edge of a scraper, which works by means of its turned-up edge biting into wood. To prepare a good edge for turning up, the sides of the blade must be perfectly flat and the edge straight, and to achieve this a fine-toothed file is used as shown in **fig B**. Obviously the file will leave scratches, and these are removed by

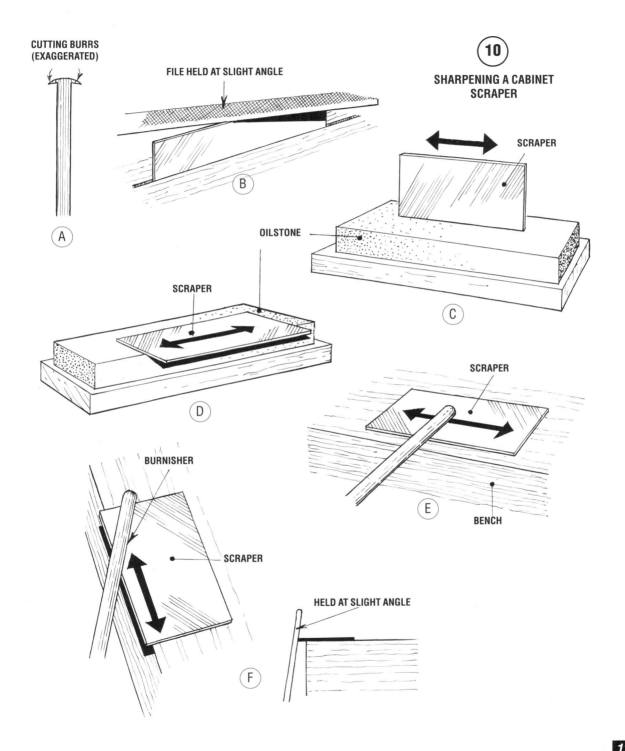

CUTTING BURRS
(EXAGGERATED)

FILE HELD AT SLIGHT ANGLE

10

**SHARPENING A CABINET
SCRAPER**

SCRAPER

B

OILSTONE

SCRAPER

C

SCRAPER

D

SCRAPER

BENCH

E

BURNISHER

SCRAPER

HELD AT SLIGHT ANGLE

F

A

rubbing the edge of the scraper on an oilstone as shown in **fig C**, followed by rubbing the scraper flat as shown in **fig D**.

The next stage involves creating 'wire edges' and you can buy a special tool called a 'burnisher' with which to do this. A knife-sharpening steel does the job as well, or you can use the back of a gouge. Whichever tool you choose, wet it and rub it hard along one of the edges a few times as shown in **fig E**.

Forming the cutting burr is the next step: hold the burnisher (or whatever tool you have chosen) at an angle slightly past the vertical and draw firmly and smoothly a few times backwards and forwards along the edge as shown in **fig F**, finally reversing the scraper to expose the other edge and repeating the action.

After some use the edge of the scraper will become too blunt to work but there is no need to go through the whole procedure as you can simply repeat the steps shown in **figs D, E** and **F** several times. Sooner or later, however, it will become obvious that the scraper needs the full re-sharpening treatment.

PLANE CUTTERS ('IRONS')

These are supplied with the edges ground at 25 degrees, which need to be sharpened to about 30 degrees by creating a burr. **Fig 11** illustrates the process. The burr, shown in **fig A**, is removed by stropping either with a leather strop or, as in **fig B**, by drawing it bevel side down across the palm of your hand and then upwards with the plain side against the palm. **Fig 12** shows the recommended shapes for the edges: as in **fig A** for smoothing planes, and in **fig B** for longer jack planes. The corners are taken off to prevent their creating ridges when flat surfaces are planed.

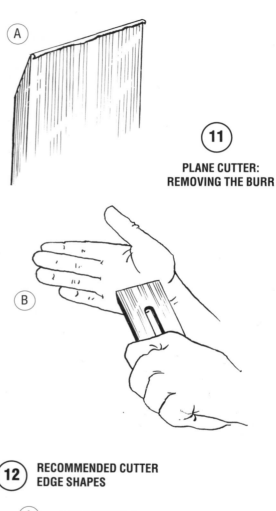

11

PLANE CUTTER: REMOVING THE BURR

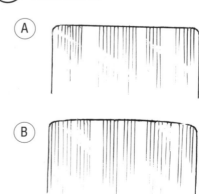

12 **RECOMMENDED CUTTER EDGE SHAPES**

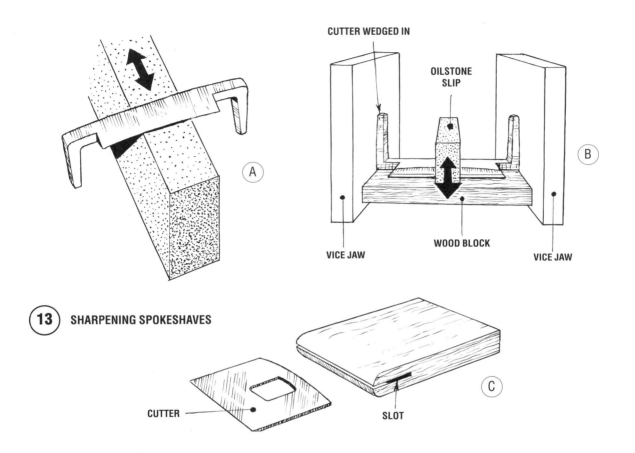

CUTTER WEDGED IN

OILSTONE SLIP

(A)

(B)

VICE JAW

WOOD BLOCK

VICE JAW

13 SHARPENING SPOKESHAVES

CUTTER

SLOT

(C)

SPOKESHAVES

Fig 13 shows three methods of sharpening spokeshaves.

There are two ways to sharpen the cutter of a wooden spokeshave and these are shown in **figs A** and **B**. The cutter in a metal spokeshave is similar to a small plane iron (see opposite), but too small to hold comfortably on an oilstone, it is jammed into a small wooden holder as shown in **fig C**.

SHARPENING STONES

OILSTONE BOX FOR USE WITH A HONING GAUGE

Many honing gauges rely on some form of roller to run back and forth on the stone, and it does not take long to wear a groove. Anyone who has had to true up an oilstone when this has happened will tell you it is a wearisome job and one to be avoided at all costs.

The device shown in **fig 14** overleaf consists

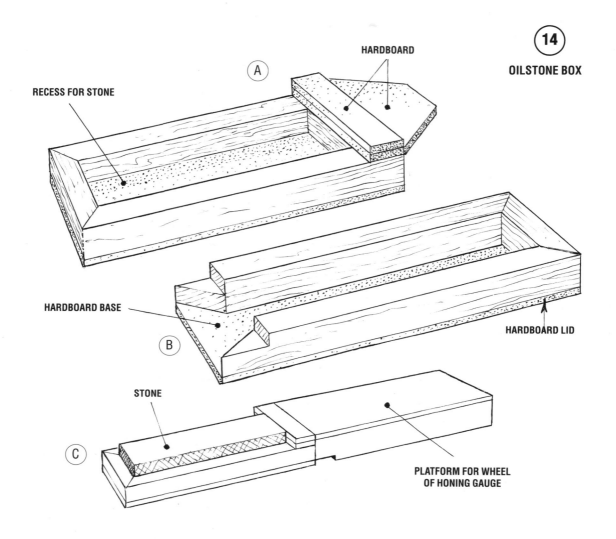

HARDBOARD

(14)

OILSTONE BOX

RECESS FOR STONE

(A)

HARDBOARD BASE

(B)

HARDBOARD LID

STONE

(C)

PLATFORM FOR WHEEL OF HONING GAUGE

of a box which holds the oilstone as a tight fit and a lid which can be taken off and butted, upside down, against the end of the box, thereby providing a flat surface for the roller of the honing gauge to run on. Oilstones vary in size and you may have to amend the dimensions shown, which fit a standard 200 x 50 x 25mm (8 x 2 x 1in) bench stone.

The main point to note is the mitred end on the box, which has a tongue glued and pinned to it as shown in **fig A**. The sides of the lid are mitred at one end to match, as shown in **fig B**. **Fig C** shows the two parts butted together: the one disadvantage is that, when the box is closed, one end of the lid is open, but this can have a piece of oiled rag pushed into it.

DIAMOND SHARPENING STONES

These are a comparatively recent innovation and they are the only stones that can sharpen both TC (tungsten-carbide) and TCT (tungsten-carbide-tipped) tools such as router cutters, planer knives and saw blades.

The monocrystalline diamonds which are used are first graded carefully and then electrolytically set into a bed of nickel, which is itself bonded to a steel plate set in a reinforced plastic base. The 'islands' on the steel plate are there to help reduce clogging and the consequent build-up of slurry.

The stones are made in several grades and are also available in various shapes and sizes, such as hand-held hones (the equivalent of oilstone slips) and bench stones. The smaller hones can be used dry or sprinkled with water, but the bench stones must always be used wet so that any slurry is flushed away. However, *all* stones must be dried thoroughly after use and stored in a dry place, and then they will last literally for a lifetime.

JAPANESE WATER STONES

These are lubricated with water in use, and in fact the coarser grit stones (from 250 to 1200 grit) need to be stored in water as they are comparatively porous. Any suitably sized plastic container will suffice; however, bear in mind that the water must not be allowed to freeze. Normally the harder 6000 and 8000 grit stones are mounted on wooden blocks and need only be sprinkled with water during use; however, all the stones are brittle and can easily be nicked or chipped unless they are handled with great care.

The stones are deliberately made so that each pass of the tool being sharpened exposes fresh abrasive, thereby giving a fast cut. This also means that if a stone becomes hollow after use it can be flattened quickly on a sheet of wet and dry paper (180 grit) laid on a flat surface, such as a piece of glass.

Chapter 7

TECHNIQUES AND ACCESSORIES FOR ASSOCIATED SKILLS

This chapter looks first at the important area of wood finishing, and surveys the choice of techniques and products available for adding the final touches to your woodworking projects. Aspects of wood-turning and veneering are also covered, plus a varied selection of other skills useful to the home woodworker.

WOOD FINISHING

USING ABRASIVES

The efficiency of abrasive paper depends on the sharpness of the particles – these are usually referred to as 'teeth' or 'grains' – and whether they are 'closed' or 'open' coats. The former brings faster results but will clog up more quickly than the latter, which lasts longer and is better suited for use on softwoods.

Among the more commonly used abrasives, aluminium oxide and silicon carbide are the hardest, followed (in sequence) by emery, garnet, silica and glass. On the back of the sheet or roll of abrasive paper you will find a 'grit' classification, which refers to the greatest number of openings in a sieve (per 25mm/1in) that the particles will pass through – thus, the higher the number, the finer the grit.

Aluminium oxide, emery and garnet abrasives range from 60 to 240 grit. For joinery work, an upper limit of 150 for painted work and 180 or 240 for a clear varnish finish is usual; cabinet work will need a finer grit up to 240 for general smoothing off. Modern polishes call for superfine grit, so that one coat can be lightly sanded prior to applying another. It is in these conditions that silicon carbide papers are ideal as their highest grade is 500 grit, while wet and dry silicon carbide is even finer at 1200 grit – it can, of course, be used wet or dry.

Glasspaper has largely been replaced by the above abrasives and is graded by an older classification: the finest grade is 000 'flour' paper, then 00, followed by 0, 1, 1½, F2, M2, 2½ and 3 (the coarsest).

The standard sheet size is 230 x 280mm (9 x 11in), and should you want to cut this into conveniently-sized pieces for hand sanding, try cutting it into three strips across its width and folding each strip into three: this will give you nine handy-sized surfaces to work with.

PREPARATION

After glasspapering the piece thoroughly by working through the grades from coarse to fine, go over it with a cloth dampened with turpentine substitute (white spirit). This will remove any grease stains (such as those from your fingers) and also pick up any microscopic dust particles that may have been ground into the surface by glasspapering, especially if you have used a mechanical sander.

When the turps has evaporated after a few minutes, sponge the work with hot water. This has two effects: it causes the wood to swell where there are hollows, thus raising it to a flat surface, and it makes any loose fibres stand up so that you can glasspaper them away when the wood is dry. This is known as 'raising the grain' and is particularly necessary on any woolly-type grain.

If there are handles, locks or other fittings, fix them on temporarily at this stage, and once you are satisfied that they fit properly, remove them. By doing this you will avoid causing any damage to the finish when the time comes finally to attach them. Any screw holes should be plugged with matching wood (see Pellets and Plugs on page 102): if they are just made good with filler, they will show as ugly spots where the filler has absorbed more stain or polish than the wood.

Filling the grain is desirable if you are using timber with comparatively open pores – oak is a good example. You can make a filler from french chalk and white (clear) french polish, or by rubbing on a paste of plaster of Paris and water or a coating of dilute glue size. However, proprietary fillers are so reasonably priced and so effective that it's not really worthwhile making your own.

A good sealer and grain filler is the shellac sealer available from all good polish suppliers which comes in a range of basic colours. Apply it with a good-quality brush such as a squirrel hair mop or a proper lacquering brush, and put on enough in the first coat for it to be absorbed evenly. Watch out for runs or puddles and brush them out immediately because the sealer dries quickly, although it takes several hours to harden completely. Once hard, paper it back with fine glasspaper and apply another coat or two, depending on how much filling is desired.

OIL FINISHES

The traditional oil finish, which was used for centuries and still is, is linseed oil. You can buy it raw or boiled, but although the latter dries more quickly it never hardens completely, so it is better to use the raw oil.

It helps if the oil can be applied warm, and because it is inflammable it is best heated in a double boiler. The warmth helps the oil to penetrate the grain, and for the first two or three coats turpentine substitute (white spirit) can be added for the same reason. Apply the oil with a cloth and work it well into the grain, wiping away any surplus. Allow it to dry before applying further coats and finish off by rubbing it with a piece of felt or a lint-free cloth, both of which must be used vigorously.

The process is never finished, as additional coats will always improve it. Remember that linseed oil does darken timber, particularly woods like cherry and walnut, and that it is resistant to practically any domestic hazard, including alcohol and water spilt on it.

Other proprietary oils are tung oil, which is obtained from the nuts of the Chinese tung tree and is discussed on page 124; Danish oil, which is a mixture of tung oil and others plus terebene driers; and teak oil, which is another blend of oils specially formulated for use on teak, a naturally greasy timber. They should all be applied in accordance with the manufacturers' instructions and to bare wood only, as sealers and grain fillers hinder the penetration.

WAX POLISH

The foregoing treatment is ideal as a basis for wax polishing and the polishes are available in a range of colours to suit pretty well all tastes. Apply the wax thinly on a pad of fine wire wool along the grain, taking care not to leave accumulations of wax around mouldings and to remove any tiny pieces of wire wool that may have broken off. Finally, buff it up with a soft lint-free duster and make a mental note to repeat the performance periodically.

FRENCH POLISHING

This is the traditional nineteenth-century finish which gives a deep, lustrous gleam to wood that is unequalled. It is not so much a complicated finish as one that can only be achieved by experience and judgement, and it is not dealt with here because until you have cultivated the sixth sense of the expert as to what to do next it can easily become a disastrous mess. In addition, it is readily marked by water, alcohol, hot cups placed on it and so on, and is unsuitable for everyday use.

However, for those interested in french polishing, a 'fad' for applying the preliminary coats of polish is highly desirable, if not essential, and the various stages in folding this simple accessory are detailed in the numbered sequence in **fig 1** – it is a good idea to practise with a piece of thick paper first.

The fad is made from a 230mm (9in) square of wadding which is soaked in polish and allowed to dry; it is then softened in methylated spirit immediately before use. This treatment will reduce the risk of loose hairs adhering to the work. A 'rubber' is a fad covered with a piece of linen or cotton fabric.

LACQUERS

There are many brands of polyurethane lacquer, which is not surprising as they are easy to apply and give a finish that is resistant to most domestic hazards. Follow the manufacturers' instructions as application is very simple.

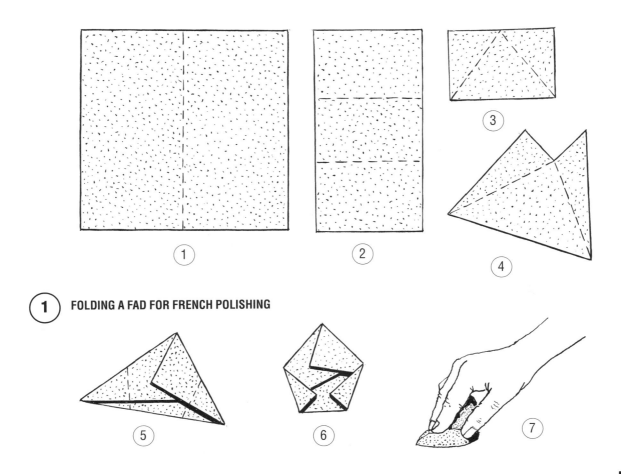

1 FOLDING A FAD FOR FRENCH POLISHING

BURNISHING

This is employed to produce what is called a 'piano' finish – in other words, a high gloss finish and one which shows up the slightest imperfection. French-polished, cellulose-lacquered and polyurethane-lacquered surfaces can all be burnished successfully, but oil and wax finishes cannot. The grain must be filled (or bodied up in the case of french polish) and the surface must be allowed to harden thoroughly.

To burnish, rub the surface with fine wet-and-dry abrasive paper wrapped around a glass-papering block. Keep a bowl of water and a bar of soap handy, and occasionally dip the paper in the water and then rub it on the soap to help as a lubricant. When you think that the surface is perfectly flat and free of any specks of dust, place the work in a good light from a window and look across it – any small imperfection can then be seen and papered down with a piece of paper held in your fingers. Before going any further, wipe the surface with a soft lint-free cloth slightly dampened with methylated spirits to pick up any dust.

The traditional method was to follow this by making a paste of Tripoli powder and water and rubbing it on with a cloth (the powder is very fine indeed and is also called 'rottenstone'). You will probably find it more convenient to use one of the proprietary burnishing creams which make the job easy and trouble-free.

FANCY OAK FINISHES

In the 1930s there was a vogue for 'novelty' finishes for oak furniture such as fuming, liming, and gold- and silver-coloured filled grain, and the method for each is described below.

Fumed oak This finish will depend on the chemical reaction between the natural tannin in the wood and ammonia fumes. In all oak finishes there is an element of chance and never more so than with fuming, so you would be well advised to experiment on a sample first. Not all oaks respond to treatment in the same degree. For example, white American oak and the red variety differ because the latter contains less tannin and does not fume so easily. Brazilian, Honduras and sapele mahogany all change colour, the first two becoming redder but flat and lifeless, and the last assuming a purple tint. Perhaps the best response of all is from chestnut, which becomes a rich brown.

If you are experimenting, try the following tips for enhancing the effect. Make a very strong pot of tea (which will contain tannin), add a couple of drops of washing-up liquid to aid penetration and wipe it over the work while the tea is still warm. Alternatively, if you can get tannin powder, mix 28g (1oz) with 1 litre (2 pints) of water and apply that; and a third suggestion is to mix 21g (¾oz) of pyrogallic powder (used in photography) with 1 litre (2 pints) of water. Using any of these mixtures will result in a more even coating of colour but they will also raise the grain, which will need to be glasspapered off.

Before fuming, remove all metal fittings and make sure that the surface is free from grease marks and any traces of glue. Arrange the work so that the fumes can circulate around it, and avoid any overlaps.

Any enclosed wooden box will do as a fuming chamber, but if you have several pieces to fume it is worth making one specially. A cabinet made up of MDF, chipboard or plywood with an up-and-down sliding door as shown in **fig 2** is ideal, and the corners and edges can be sealed with an adhesive tape. The cabinet should fit as closely to the work as possible so

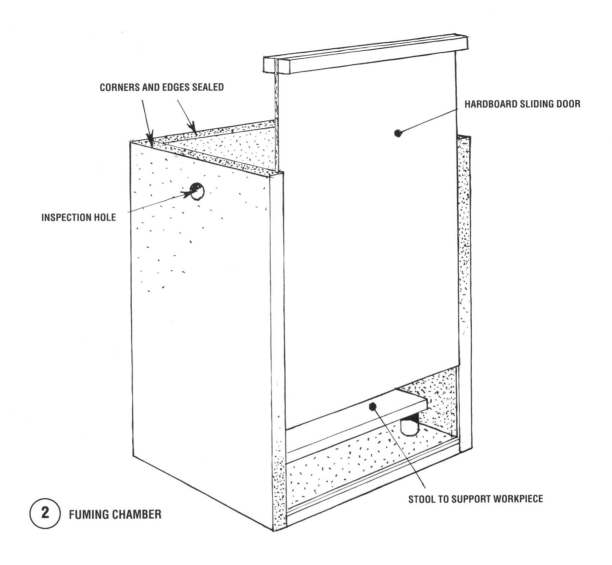

CORNERS AND EDGES SEALED

HARDBOARD SLIDING DOOR

INSPECTION HOLE

STOOL TO SUPPORT WORKPIECE

2 FUMING CHAMBER

that the fumes are concentrated. Make a small hole towards the top through which you can insert a piece of rod or dowel made from the same wood as the work being fumed: this can be withdrawn from time to time to check progress. A flat base of MDF or similar board with a length of dowel glued in at each corner as a leg will make a good stand to support the work inside the box and to allow the fumes to circulate.

There are several grades of ammonia and the '880' grade supplied by polish manufacturers is reckoned to be the most effective; the others are used in household cleaners and are weaker. Oak will change colour quite rapidly – sometimes in less than an hour – so frequent checks are needed. The ammonia should be poured into one or more saucers which are then placed in the cabinet, and you will need to check after a few hours or so to see if they need replenishment. This is where the sliding door is handy, as the job needs to be done quickly. The fumes are dangerous to the lungs and eyes and you should wear a respirator, eye protection and rubber gloves. When the process is complete, a solution of bichromate of potash in water can be applied to match up uneven patches.

Do not be tempted to use a transparent plastic bag instead of a cabinet (as is sometimes suggested), as any kind of light will have a deleterious effect on the process.

Liming In the old days this was a messy business, as it involved slaking unslaked lime and stirring it with a stick until it resembled a thick paint, which was then rubbed into the grain with an old rag or piece of sacking.

Today the job is made much easier by using a proprietary liming paste, although there are several conditions to fulfil to be sure of success, the principal one being a surface that is free of all imperfections as the paste will exaggerate the smallest blemish.

Although oak is the traditional timber to receive the treatment, any open-grained wood is suitable; in fact, it usually helps to open up the grain on all of them by wire-brushing lightly along the grain. One of the small wire brushes used on suede shoes is preferable to the large workshop type, which do tend to be somewhat brutal.

The next step is to decide what basic colour you want the oak to be, and there is an enormous range of coloured water stains from which to choose. Whichever you use, it will raise the grain, so the procedure is to apply the stain liberally, wait an hour or so and then glasspaper the surface lightly. Follow this by applying a couple of coats of sanding sealer, which must be allowed to dry thoroughly, and preferably overnight.

Now apply the liming paste with a cloth, rubbing it vigorously across the grain until the pores are filled, then remove the excess paste before it dries. A wax polish finish is best and as a bonus it will help to remove any paste that has dried on hard – what you must avoid is using any finish that is based on methylated or white spirit, which may begin to lift the paste unless it is put on very carefully.

Gold and silver finishes These finishes are achieved by using proprietary pastes instead of liming paste – otherwise, the procedure is the same. You can make your own gold and silver pastes by adding the appropriate powder to some glue size (which acts as a binder) until you have a thick paste, which will have to be thinned with turps to make it workable. You will need to test it from time to time on a piece of scrap wood to gauge the effect. Rub the paste on across the grain with a piece of wadding or fine wire wool so that it remains in the grain, and then wipe off the excess using a soft lint-free rag.

FINISH FOR WOOD IN CONTACT WITH FOOD

By far the best finish is pure tung oil (also called 'Chinese wood oil') as it is completely non-toxic, waterproof and will not taint food by taste or smell. It is only suitable for bare wood, which means that any previous finish must be removed completely, as must any sealer or filler.

Apply two or three coats, depending on the

absorbency of the wood, diluting each coat 50/50 with turpentine substitute (white spirit) and allow to dry for 24–48 hours between each coat. Rub in the oil vigorously with a cloth and wipe off the surplus, and when dry rub the surface lightly with finest-grade wire wool to remove the film which would otherwise hinder the absorption of subsequent coats.

Finally, finish with a coat of undiluted oil and allow several days for it to harden before rubbing with wire wool as before. If necessary, you can freshen the surface from time to time with a coat of diluted oil.

Tung oil is also a first-class treatment for use outdoors on garden furniture and other items.

MISCELLANEOUS MATERIALS

Beaumontage This is a home-made stopping that can be coloured to match the wood perfectly. There are, of course, dozens of proprietary stoppings and fillers which give good results, but rarely an exact match.

To make beaumontage, mix equal parts of beeswax, powder colour and crushed resin thoroughly with a few broken-up flakes of shellac and warm the mixture gently in a tin until it melts. Before it hardens completely, roll it in your hands into the shape of a thick stick.

To use the beaumontage, press it against a pre-heated metal rod so that it melts and runs down to fill the blemish, as shown in **fig 3**. Overfill the blemish slightly so that you can cut off the beaumontage flush with the surface using a wet chisel. Remember: the colour must match the wood after this has been stained, as the beaumontage itself will not absorb stain.

Bichromate of potash When made into a solution, this is still one of the most popular stains for home use. It is purchased as reddish orange

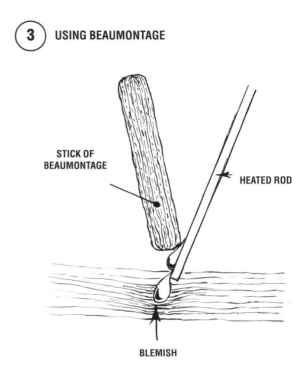

3 USING BEAUMONTAGE

STICK OF BEAUMONTAGE

HEATED ROD

BLEMISH

crystals which are dissolved in water – it is best to make up a concentrated solution from which you can take small amounts for further dilution, because the effect can only be judged by experimenting on the actual wood being stained. The strength of the reaction depends on the amount of tannin in the wood, and as you would expect, oak is the usual timber to be treated, followed by mahogany: the solution has no effect on softwoods. Oak is darkened and takes on a slightly greenish brown tint, while mahogany becomes a cold, deep brown.

Borax An alkaline white powder, borax can be dissolved in water and used to neutralize the effect of oxalic acid and some other bleaches.

Crocus powder This very fine powder, which is obtained from calcined metal, is used as an abrasive to dull down a shiny finish.

Oxalic acid Sometimes used as a bleach in the proportion of 50g (2oz) to 300ml (½ pint) of hot water, which can be diluted as required, oxalic acid is poisonous and you should protect your hands and eyes. Wash down the work with a borax solution (see above) followed by fresh water to remove all traces.

Permanganate of potash These purple crystals can be dissolved in water to produce a rich brown stain. Although often recommended, its colour is fugitive and cannot be guaranteed permanent.

Shellac Shellac is derived from the sticky juice exuded by the lac insect found in India, which is refined and then formed into flakes, or 'buttons'. When dissolved in alcohol or methylated spirit, it becomes french polish; it is also invaluable as a first-coat sealer for all non-greasy timbers and will accept all finishes except those with a water base. Shellac is particularly recommended as a primer for use before wax polishing, as it will prevent dirt entering the grain.

Sulphate of iron (green copperas) This is used to kill the redness of mahogany so that it resembles walnut more closely; it also gives oak a blue-grey tint. 'Harewood' is sycamore which assumes a light grey colour when it is treated with sulphate of iron. This can be bought in garden centres, as it is a well-known moss killer.

Turpentine When pure, this is an oleoresin which oozes from certain kinds of trees when they are cut or slashed – the terebinth tree is one of the main sources. Now expensive, it is usually available from art suppliers. Turpentine substitute (white spirit) is a different substance and is produced by distilling some of the by-products from processing softwoods.

WOODTURNING LATHE

Even in the middle price range, a lathe is one of the most expensive woodworking machines and you need to study as many as you can before parting with your money. These are some of the main points to consider:

- The various components such as head- and tailstocks, bed, tool rest and accessories like swivelling heads and chucks must all be perfectly rigid when assembled, otherwise you will be working with a handicap from the very start.
- Do not assume that one manufacturer's accessories will fit another's lathe – even though it may be more expensive, it is advisable to choose a manufacturer who can supply all the extras you may need.
- The majority of lathes are supplied already bolted to a stand, but there are also machines without stands that can be fixed to your own bench; in any case, those that are fitted to stands can be unbolted and bench-mounted. This can be important if you are under or over average height, as you must feel comfortable and in control: the correct working height can be found by bending your arm close to your body and measuring the distance from your elbow to the floor. Deduct 38mm (1½in) from this measurement to arrive at the correct height for the centre line of the lathe.

- Some lathes have three, and others four, speeds varying from 450rpm to 2500rpm. These are adjusted by moving the belt drive from the motor on to pulleys of different sizes – unless the lathe is fitted with a variomatic control, when a single switch does the job.
- The length between centres, which is the effective distance you can turn, generally ranges between 730mm (28in) and 990mm (39in), which should be adequate unless you are contemplating turning extra-long work such as lamp standards.
- Check that the headstock and tailstock are precisely in line both when viewed from above and horizontally, otherwise accurate work will be difficult.
- The tool rest must be robust and capable of adjustment, so that you can turn close to the workpiece and also lower the rest below the centre line if necessary.
- The final critical dimension is the maximum diameter that can be turned without hitting the bed bars and this is usually about 300mm (11¾in): on some machines you can swivel the headstock through 90 degrees and turn much larger diameters such as large bowls by using a bowl-turning attachment (an extra accessory).

JIGS FOR WOODTURNING

1 HOLDING TURNED WORK FOR POLISHING, VARNISHING ETC

The figure shows a cradle holding turned work. The upright pieces are made from one strip of wood which has slots of the required size bored centrally along it; it is then sawn in half along its length.

Carved pieces and mouldings can be held down on a piece of scrap wood by means of double-sided adhesive tape, which allows them to be removed easily when dry.

2 STEADY FOR VASE TURNING

The problem here is to hold the blank firmly while hollowing it, as obviously the tailstock gets in the way and prevents the job being done between centres.

To overcome this, you can make up a steady as shown. The upright parts can be jigsawn from MDF and then the slots for the wing nuts routed out. The bottom block needs to be more substantial and is screwed and glued to the uprights; a hole is drilled through the block to accept a T-bolt, which engages in the slot in the lathe saddle.

In use, the steady is placed in position and the tailstock brought up to it so that the work can be aligned correctly and the steady and sliding pieces adjusted. The tailstock is then removed and hollowing out can be started – remember to rub a little wax on to the work where the slides touch it so that the wood does not burn.

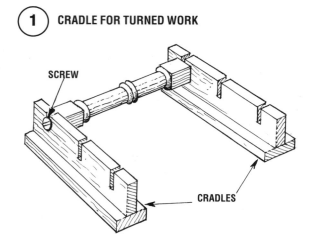

1 CRADLE FOR TURNED WORK

SCREW

CRADLES

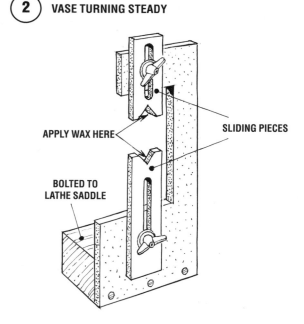

2 VASE TURNING STEADY

APPLY WAX HERE

SLIDING PIECES

BOLTED TO LATHE SADDLE

3 LOOSENING A JAMMED FACEPLATE

Jamming sometimes occurs with a new machine, as the faceplate collects heat from the bearing when in use and expands slightly: it then tightens a little more on the mandrel, and when the machine is switched off for any length of time it contracts again and jams tight.

All faceplates have holes in them for the work to be screwed on, and if you screw on a batten instead, as shown, you can give this a few hammer blows to loosen the plate.

4 HOME-MADE WOODEN CHUCKS

Each of the chucks shown can be screwed on to a standard woodscrew chuck.

The chuck shown in **fig A** is a 'collet' chuck. It consists of a hollow cup with a solid end which is fixed on to the woodscrew chuck. The work is jammed into it and is further tightened by

(3) LOOSENING A JAMMED FACEPLATE

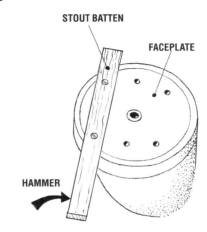

driving a tapered wooden pin across it at right angles – it helps if a small 'flat' can be made on the work for the pin to bear against.

The chuck shown in **fig B** also consists of a wooden cup, but this one is slightly tapered and

(4) HOME-MADE CHUCKS

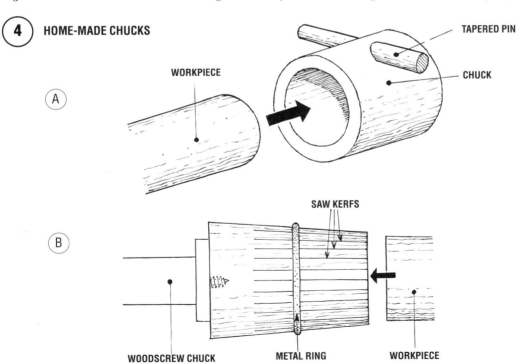

has a number of slits cut partway down its length. The work is fitted inside it and a metal collar is driven along the taper to tighten up the whole thing.

5 OFF-CENTRE TURNING

Accomplished woodturners may like to try this kind of turning, which is sometimes found on the older style of chair backfeet. The snag is, of course, that the backfoot cannot be turned in the conventional manner because of the angle of the lower part of the leg.

To overcome this, you need to make the jig a shown in **fig A**, which is cramped to the backfoot as shown in **fig B**. The jig is centred on the headstock and a screw is inserted through the step on the underside into the end of the backfoot to steady it, while its other end is centred on the tailstock in the usual way.

The trick is to know what size to make the jig, as you don't want anything too heavy whizzing round at high speed in the lathe, so it is a matter of trial, error and experience.

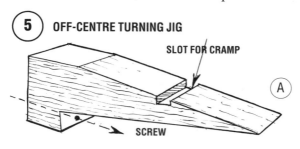

5 OFF-CENTRE TURNING JIG

SLOT FOR CRAMP

Ⓐ

SCREW

VENEERS

There are four different methods of producing veneers – sawn, knife cut, rotary cut and half-rotary cut – and the last three are shown in **fig 1**. Sawcut veneers, which are the thickest, are used mainly by furniture restorers and are sold by specialist suppliers, while rotary cut veneers, shown in **fig A**, are used mainly for plywood. The two that concern us are the knife cut, shown in **fig B**, which produces most of the veneers on sale, and the half-rotary cut, shown in **fig C**, which is used for highly figured and exotic veneers.

Ideally, all veneers should be stored flat on shelves in a dark cellar where the temperature and humidity do not vary very much: few of us can provide this environment, and keeping the veneers flat and covered with a sheet of cardboard under the bed in the spare bedroom is as near as we can get, particularly if the central heating is kept as low as possible.

Sawcut veneer can be up to 2mm (¹⁄₁₆in) thick – in fact, you can saw it yourself if only small pieces are required – but commercial veneers are usually about 0.5mm (¹⁄₃₂in), although exotics can be even thinner.

Techniques and devices for cutting and preparing veneers ready for use are described on page 134.

Caul veneering Many woodworkers like to veneer their own boards and one of the most

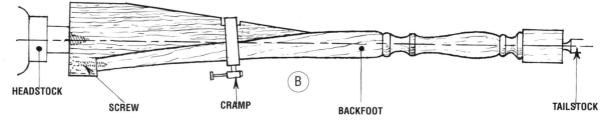

HEADSTOCK

SCREW

CRAMP

Ⓑ

BACKFOOT

TAILSTOCK

1 VENEER CUTTING METHODS

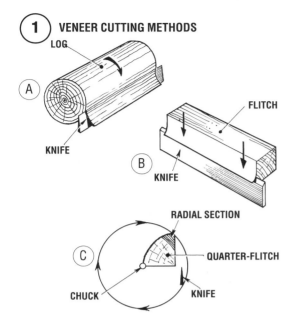

LOG

A

KNIFE

FLITCH

B

KNIFE

RADIAL SECTION

C

QUARTER-FLITCH

CHUCK

KNIFE

effective ways of doing this is by caul veneering. **Fig 2** shows a typical set-up which comprises upper and lower bearers, strips of hardboard to prevent bruising, the caul (which is a sheet of stout timber), G-cramps, and of course the workpiece itself.

The figure is self-explanatory: the most important point is that the upper bearer (but not the lower) must be very slightly curved on its underside, so that the tightening of the cramps ensures that pressure is applied to the centre first to avoid any likelihood of trapped air bubbles.

Fig 3 overleaf shows three ways of using simple cauls for holding the veneer on to shaped surfaces: **figs A** and **B** are self-explanatory, but

fig C is more complicated. Here the box is simply a container for the sand bag, which is cotton or canvas – not plastic – and holds sand that has been warmed on a tray in the oven. A rough hollow should be scooped out, and then the workpiece with the glued veneer fixed to it temporarily with elastic bands is placed in it and a block placed on top; the whole thing is then cramped together. There are two points to note: first, a sheet of newspaper is interposed between the work and the bag, and should it adhere it can be removed with a damp cloth afterwards; second, the sand is warmed only to prevent the glue from chilling and should not be really hot.

If you are contemplating veneering much shaped work, relatively inexpensive vacuum bag presses are available, where the pressure of a vacuum pulls a rubber blanket down over the veneer and the work. A vacuum pump exhausts the air, and although you can try to simulate it by using an ordinary domestic vacuum cleaner and a plastic bag, this is not quite

2 CAUL VENEERING SET-UP

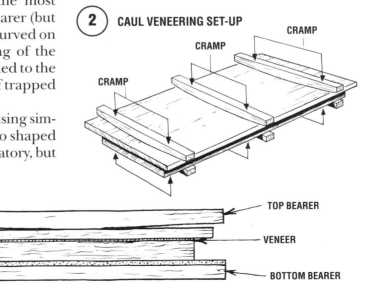

CRAMP

CRAMP

CRAMP

CRAMP

CAUL

GROUNDWORK

TOP BEARER

VENEER

BOTTOM BEARER

3 CAUL VENEERING ON SHAPED SURFACES

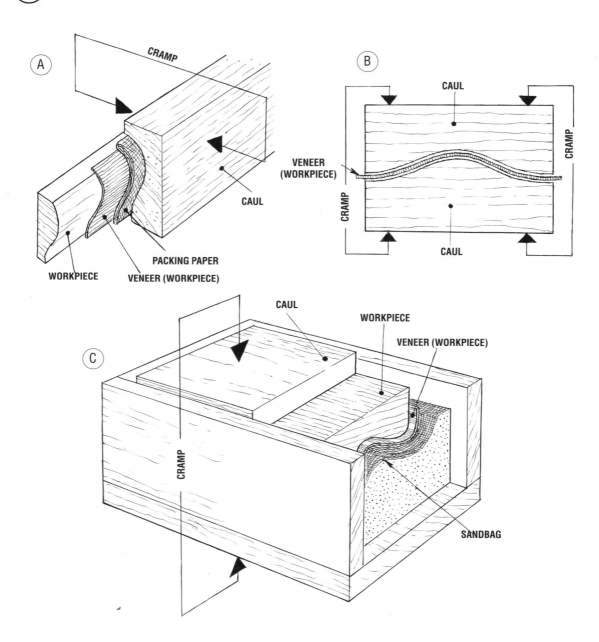

A · CRAMP · CAUL · WORKPIECE · PACKING PAPER · VENEER (WORKPIECE)

B · CAUL · CRAMP · VENEER (WORKPIECE) · CRAMP · CAUL

C · CAUL · WORKPIECE · VENEER (WORKPIECE) · CRAMP · SANDBAG

as straightforward as it may appear at first sight.

Fig 4 shows a set-up with which you could experiment. The outer bag must be one which will not tear or rip easily but is also flexible, and could be one of the type sold in garden centres for carrying garden rubbish. There are several points to bear in mind. First, the workpiece is, of course, introduced through the open end of the bag, which needs to be held tightly closed afterwards. The simplest way to do this is to clamp the end between two battens as shown, or you could attach Velcro around the mouth of the bag.

At the other end there has to be some means of connecting the hose of the vacuum cleaner so that it can exhaust the air. You can buy a garden hose fitting for joining lengths of hoses end to end which incorporates a tap, and by cutting a hole in the end of the bag to fit tightly over one of the threaded parts of the fitting, followed by a washer cut from a piece of spare rubber (pond liner is ideal), and then clamping everything together with the collar, you can achieve an airtight seal. A suitable hose is pushed on to the outside part of the fitting, another washer is added, and once the collar has been tightened it can be then fixed to the vacuum cleaner.

Obviously the workpiece must rest on something which has to be perforated so that all the air can be exhausted, and a grid made up of criss-crossed wooden beading with all sharp edges and corners removed should do the job. Before putting the workpiece inside, the veneer must be held in place temporarily with elastic bands or nylon elasticated thread.

 HOME-MADE VACUUM BAG PRESS

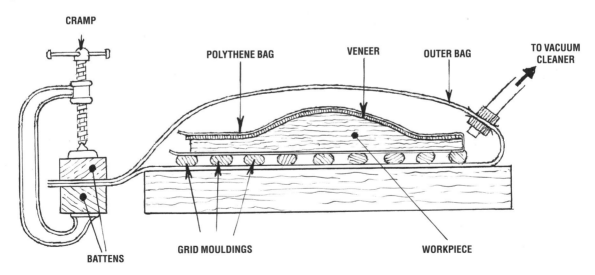

VENEERING TECHNIQUES AND DEVICES

1 CUTTING EDGES STRAIGHT

The three most practical ways to cut the edges of veneers straight so they are ready for laying are shown here. In the first, shown in **fig A**, a small razor saw (as used by model makers) cuts against a batten which is cramped to a wooden block, with one or more veneers sandwiched between them. Or you can buy a veneer saw as shown in **fig B**: the way to use it is obvious. Note the curved edge, which means there is no sharp point on the blade that could dig in. In addition, the teeth have no set, so the saw can be used tight against a guide batten.

In **fig C**, a chisel (or alternatively a craft knife) is used against a straightedge, which not only acts as a guide but prevents the veneer from buckling – note the batten, which is used as a support.

2 CUTTING SMALL-RADIUS CURVES

Things begin to get trickier when small-radius curves have to be cut. The method shown uses a pair of dividers to do most of the cutting. One leg is positioned on a piece of scrap veneer which has the centre of the curve marked on it, and the other leg scribes it on the actual veneer – you could sharpen this leg so that it makes a deep scratch, which could be followed by cutting with a knife. The scrap piece can be used as a template for the other corners.

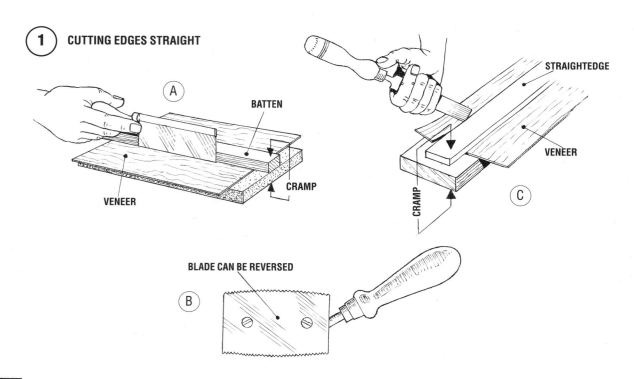

1 CUTTING EDGES STRAIGHT

A
BATTEN
CRAMP
VENEER

STRAIGHTEDGE
VENEER
CRAMP
C

BLADE CAN BE REVERSED
B

(2) CUTTING SMALL-RADIUS CURVES

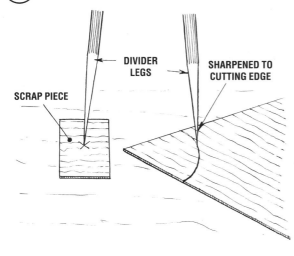

DIVIDER LEGS

SHARPENED TO CUTTING EDGE

SCRAP PIECE

disastrous, however, as they can be butted together when glued down and the joint will be practically invisible.

The recommended method is to use a cutting gauge as shown. Note that the straightedge (which could be a batten) in no way acts as a guide for the gauge but serves merely to hold down the veneer to prevent it from buckling. The face of the gauge fence runs along and is guided by the edge of the veneer, and for this reason the batten is allowed to overhang by 3mm (⅛in) or so. There is no need to buy a cutting gauge especially for a one-off job, as you can replace the pin of a marking gauge by a nail with its point sharpened to a chisel edge.

3 CUTTING CROSSBANDINGS

This process can be difficult, as you are cutting across the grain and, as far as possible, the banding should remain in one piece. If it does break into several pieces it is not completely

4 TRIMMING EDGES

Trimming the edge of a veneer leaf usually involves holding it down with a batten on a shooting board with its edge overhanging very slightly and shooting it with a finely set plane.

(3) CUTTING CROSSBANDINGS

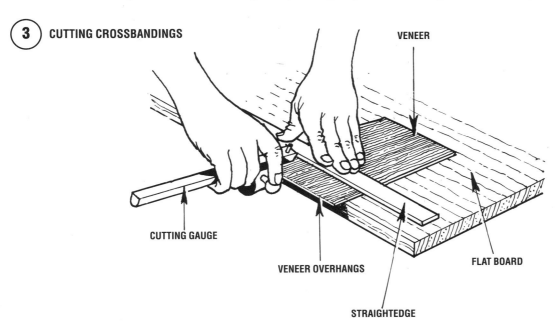

VENEER

CUTTING GAUGE

VENEER OVERHANGS

STRAIGHTEDGE

FLAT BOARD

(**4**)   **TRIMMING EDGES**

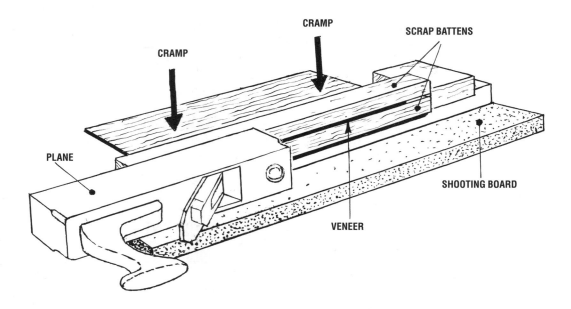

Sometimes, however, the veneer edge will persist in crumbling away, and to overcome this you should cramp it between two pieces of scrap batten as shown, so that its edge is flush with theirs. Then take a shaving or two off the face of the battens and, of course, the edge of the veneer. Several leaves can be cramped between two battens and the whole package planed on a shooting board.

5 CUTTING SHAPES AROUND A TEMPLATE

Cutting out curved designs such as circles or ellipses can be awkward, and **figs A** and **B** show two kinds of knife which should make things easier. The knife in **fig A** can be ground from an old table knife: it has a relatively small point ground on the end so that the whole width of the blade supports the point while it is being pressed down. The familiar craft knife shown

in **fig B** is a reasonable alternative if you hold it at a steep angle while cutting. A scalpel is unsuitable, as the point can easily break off.

Do not try to cut around a thick template as it will hinder the knife point as you follow it – use something as thin as is consistent with the rigidity needed. Metal is an obvious choice but can be difficult to work; 3mm (⅛in) Perspex is good if you are only cutting a few pieces, and you can see the marked line easily.

(**5**)   **KNIVES FOR CUTTING OUT SHAPES**

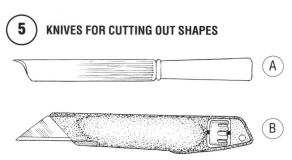

6 KEEPING VENEERS FLAT

A major problem is keeping the veneers flat while they are waiting to be used. A well-tried and proven method is to dampen each leaf lightly with glue size and then sandwich it between two boards – chipboard would be suitable, but not MDF. Then place a heavy weight on top and leave overnight; the leaf should then be dry and flat enough to use the next morning. You could, of course, make a whole stack of 'sandwiches', provided the leaves are separated by boards between each.

7 VENEERING HAMMER

Details of the construction of one of these are shown in the figure. The dimensions are only a guide and any variation will make little difference. The blade can be made from brass, hard plastic, or any hardwood.

8 MAKING YOUR OWN BANDINGS

Bandings are often seen on modern furniture in the form of crossbandings, which are borders of veneer, usually about 25mm (1in) wide, with the grain running crosswise.

It is quite simple to make your own bandings and use up offcuts in the process. **Fig A** shows how to do it: a series of strips of a darker veneer have been glued between the blocks at regular intervals to give a more attractive finished appearance.

The blocks must be of the same thickness, as they will eventually be sawn across the grain to give crossgrained 'slices' or bandings. Glue the blocks together edge to edge and leave them on a baseboard with a weighted board on top while the adhesive sets. Remember to interpose the waxed paper or plastic film, which will prevent any surplus adhesive from sticking to the baseboard and spoiling the job.

Gluing a face veneer above and below the blocks as shown in **fig B** will give you the patterned banding in **fig C**. By incorporating blocks and veneers of different woods and different colours, you can build up some very attractive patterns.

(8) **MAKING BANDINGS**

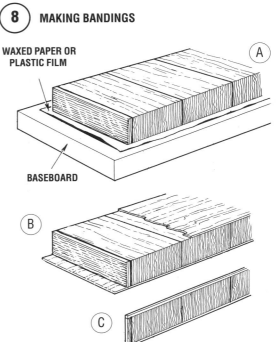

WAXED PAPER OR
PLASTIC FILM

A

BASEBOARD

B

C

(7) **VENEERING HAMMER**

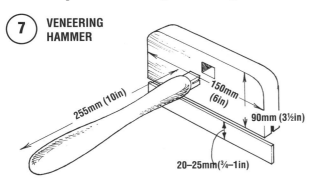

255mm (10in)

150mm (6in)

90mm (3½in)

20–25mm(¾–1in)

9 MAKING HERRINGBONE BANDINGS

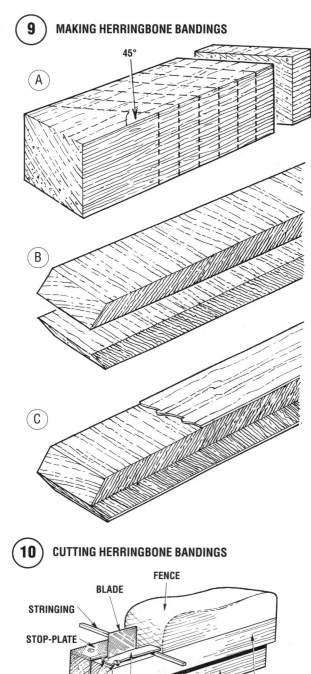

A word of warning: always make up about double the amount of blocks compared to the combined thicknesses of the finished bandings, as each sawcut will remove roughly the same amount of wood in sawdust as does the banding you are cutting off.

9 MAKING HERRINGBONE BANDINGS

The above method can be adapted to make herringbone bandings. In **fig A**, the block is sawn across at 45 degrees to give 'slices' of the requisite thickness. These are juxtaposed, with the grain opposed at 90 degrees as shown in **fig B**. Finally, the slices are glued up as shown in **fig C** (remembering to place them on the waxed paper or plastic film) – the outer veneers are, of course, optional.

10 CUTTING HERRINGBONE BANDINGS

Herringbone bandings can be purchased in a wide variety of colours, woods and patterns, and widths ranging from 0.6mm to 6mm (1/32 to 1/4in); they are usually square in section.

The figure shows a device for cutting these bandings that can be made in the workshop, using a piece of sharpened cabinet scraper steel or a broken bandsaw blade as a cutter. The wood should be sawn and planed as near to the required size as possible, and may be finished off by being pulled through the device against the cutter.

11 SCRATCH STOCK

Although most grooves can be worked using a power router fitted with a standard veining cutter, there inevitably comes a time when you have no suitable cutter or it is just too expensive to buy one specially for a one-off job. In such circumstances the scratch stock comes into its own, and this device is easily made in the workshop.

The design shown here is an improvement on those usually recommended, which have fences that are too small. The fence can be made from two pieces of plywood or MDF, each cut into an L-shape to enclose the stem; a wing nut clamps them in place. A small slot needs to be cut right through the stem as near to the end as possible and this should be the correct size to contain the two cutters with a tiny wedge-shaped shim between them, plus another wedge which will hold them all in place when it is tapped in. Remember that the actual lining needs to fit tightly in its groove, so the cutters must be spaced accordingly.

If a hole is bored at the opposite end to accept an ordinary woodscrew, its point can rotate on a packing piece, which is fastened to the top of the bench with double-sided adhesive tape. The device can then be employed to cut curved grooves by adjusting the fence to the appropriate radius and using another packing piece to bring it level with the surface of the workpiece.

12 HOLDING INLAID BANDINGS IN PLACE

It is sometimes difficult to hold inlaid bandings in position on an edge while the adhesive sets, because they are flexible and tend to spring out of the rebate. The method shown in **fig 12** below solves the problem.

Battens are cramped above and below the work a few centimetres away from the edge, and small nails or pins are driven into them at frequent intervals. A length of dampened string is then passed around them as shown and will pull the line tightly home as it dries.

12   **HOLDING INLAID BANDINGS IN PLACE**

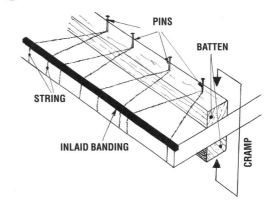

11   **IMPROVED SCRATCH STOCK**

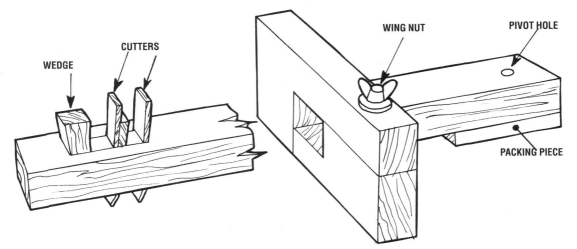

ASSOCIATED TECHNIQUES

1 LAYING LEATHER FLAT

This technique is employed when laying leather on a flat surface such as the writing flap of a bureau. Specially prepared sheepskin called a 'skiver' is used for this type of work; because the leather comes from a sheep, the size is necessarily limited to about 840 x 610mm (33 x 24in). Larger sizes involve joining two pieces together and this particular job is best left to the supplier.

The first step is to lay the leather on the work and centralize it, as the supplier will have left a margin for trimming. This will also enable you to adjust the fit to take into account any tooling on the edges. This done, run your thumbnail along the longest edge of the recess to make an indentation and then cut along it.

To stick down the leather, use PVA woodworking adhesive diluted in the proportion four parts adhesive to one part cold water. Apply it all over the recess and insert the long edge you have just cut tight up to the edge. Press it down with a clean soft cloth, and then rub gently and firmly in the directions shown by the arrows. Leather tends to have a natural stretch and you should aim for a taut surface, not only free from air bubbles, but also from any excessive tension.

You will need a really sharp craft knife for trimming the remaining edges. Run around the edges of the recess with your fingernail to press the leather home, and then trim around it with the tip of the craft knife blade. As the leather has been dyed, it is important that the edge is undercut to hide the difference in colour. In addition, you should keep the blade twisted at a slight angle so that it tends to cut towards the wood rather than the leather.

Corners can be tricky, and the best way to deal with them is to hold the waste leather out of the way at right angles and make the next cut into the corner from the opposite direction.

Finally, press the edges down with your thumbnail and leave the work to dry. However, it is worth coming back after half an hour or so to rub out any bubbles or wrinkles that may have developed.

1 LAYING LEATHER FLAT

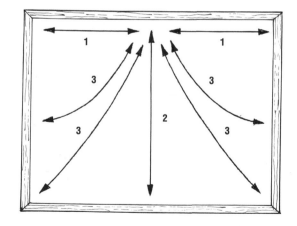

2 STRETCHING WEBBING

This is properly done with a webbing strainer, but provided the frame to be webbed is free and can be held on the bench, you can tack the web in place on one end and then stand the frame on the bench as shown and press it downwards and backwards. As the loose end of the web is gripped in the vice, it is easy to strain it before tacking it and cutting it off.

3 USING PLASTIC FOAM

Cutting plastic foam neatly can be a problem, although there is a selection of tools with which to do it. It is possible to use scissors or a sharp kitchen knife, but the best of all is an electric carving knife, which makes the job a pleasure. Next best is a sharp craft knife, although it can be difficult to cut thick pieces neatly.

Figs A–D overleaf show how to cut some

2 STRETCHING WEBBING

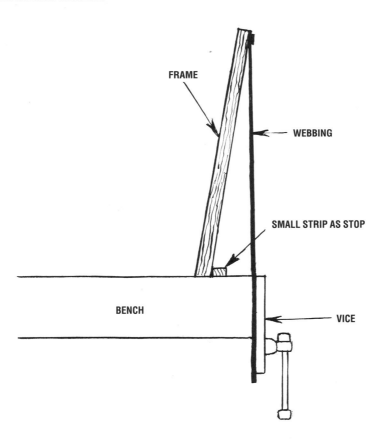

FRAME

WEBBING

SMALL STRIP AS STOP

BENCH

VICE

3 CUTTING PLASTIC FOAM

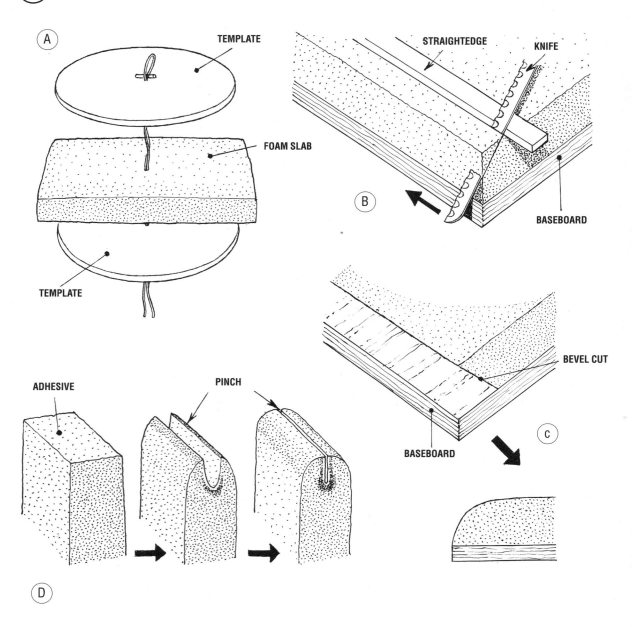

A — TEMPLATE, FOAM SLAB, TEMPLATE

B — STRAIGHTEDGE, KNIFE, BASEBOARD

C — BEVEL CUT, BASEBOARD

D — ADHESIVE, PINCH

basic shapes. **Fig A** shows how two circular templates can be used to guide you when cutting a disc. These can be made from hardboard or stout cardboard, with a hole bored in the exact centre of each. A length of strong twine is then looped through the assembly as shown and a small stick is inserted through the loop. Tying off the ends tightly will give you a 'sandwich' that can be cut accurately.

Fig B shows the straightforward process of cutting a bevel. All you need to do is hold the knife blade at a constant angle, using the straightedge as a guide. A similar procedure, shown in **fig C**, will produce a rounded edge. The edge of the foam is undercut at an angle as shown, and the overhang is then stuck down.

To produce a bullnose edge, try the method shown in **fig D**. Apply adhesive to the edge, allow it to become tacky and then pinch it together as shown.

Chapter *8*

MEASURING, MARKING
AND BASIC GEOMETRY

Accurate woodworking depends on accurate measuring and marking, and this chapter offers a host of techniques, tips and devices which will help you to achieve this and produce professional-looking results every time.

TECHNIQUES AND DEVICES FOR MEASURING AND MARKING

1 TAKING ACCURATE MEASUREMENTS

The first rule is to remember the old adage 'Measure twice and cut once', which is as true today as it ever was.

When measuring with a ruler, if possible stand it on edge as shown in **fig A** – using it flat, as shown in **fig B**, can give small discrepancies unless your eyes are exactly above the mark.

Sooner or later you will need to cut several pieces of identical length from one longer piece. Cut the first piece precisely true and then use it as a template for marking the others. This is more accurate than using a ruler to measure each one.

1   TAKING ACCURATE MEASUREMENTS

RIGHT

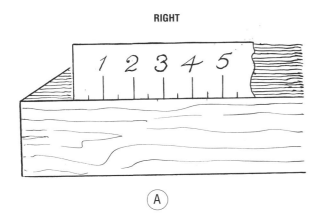

WRONG

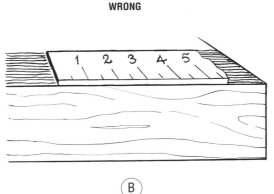

A

B

2 SPACING CALCULATOR

This simple device provides a quick way to divide straight lines of various lengths into equal parts.

Fig A shows how to make it: mine is made from a piece of white-enamelled hardboard approximately 460 x 380mm (18 x 15in), which is a convenient size. I first scored the lines with a marking knife very carefully and then went over them with a ballpoint pen. **Fig B** shows that a piece of wood placed anywhere across the lines will automatically be divided into equal parts, and by moving it back and forth the parts can be made greater or smaller.

3 MARKING OUT EQUAL DIVISIONS

Often when constructing a carcase for a sideboard or a set of cupboards you will need to mark out vertical partitions that are equally spaced.

The figure shows an easy way to do this which takes into account the thickness of the partitions themselves.

The thicknesses of the intermediate partitions are marked out from one end of the carcase and the distance from **a** to **b** is then divided into three, giving the measurement for three equal divisions.

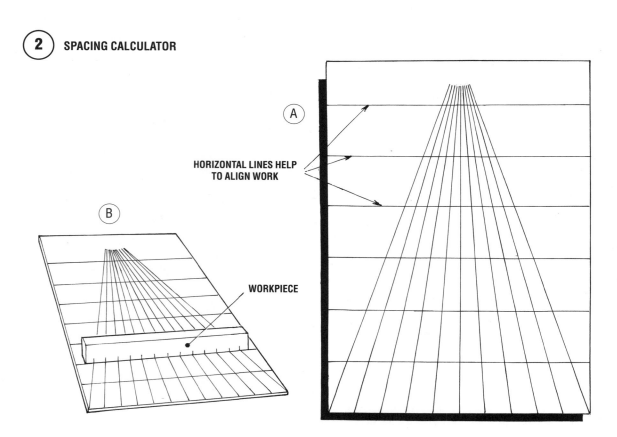

2 SPACING CALCULATOR

A

HORIZONTAL LINES HELP
TO ALIGN WORK

B

WORKPIECE

3 **MARKING OUT EQUAL DIVISIONS**

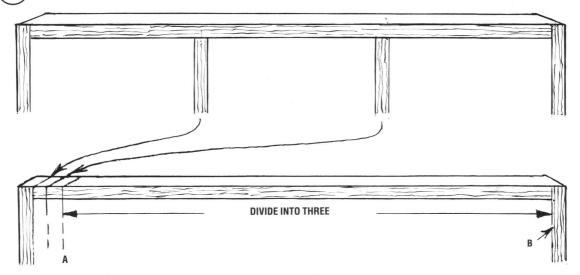

4 CENTRING SQUARE

This device is best made from offcuts of 2mm (1⁄16in) acrylic sheet, but hardboard or thin plywood could also be used.

The first job is to mark out the cross shown by the dotted lines **ab** and **cd**. The lengths can be whatever is convenient, but 65mm (2½in) and 130mm (5in) would be suitable, and the distance **cx** could be 25mm (1in). The two pins are inserted at equal distances from **x**; the rounded shape at the top is purely decorative.

To use the device, locate the pins on the circumference of the cylinder end or disc and mark a line following the straight edge; then move it to another position and mark a second line. The point where the lines intersect will be the centre.

4 **CENTRING SQUARE**

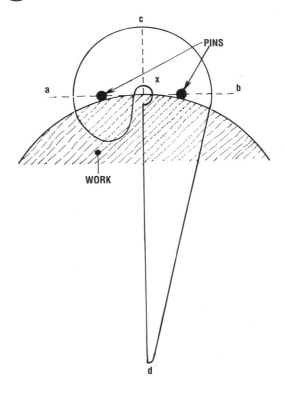

5 BISECTING LINES AND ANGLES

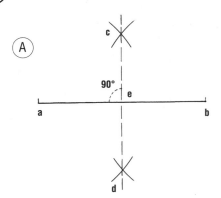

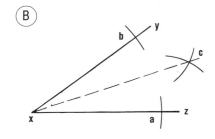

5 BISECTING LINES AND ANGLES

Figs A and **B** show how to cut a line or an angle in half (bisecting).

In **fig A**, the ends of the line are marked **a** and **b** and a pair of compasses centred on these points is used with any suitable angle to draw the arcs as shown. A line joining the points **c** and **d** where the arcs intersect will bisect the line **ab** and will also be at right angles to it.

In **fig B**, the lines forming the angle to be bisected are marked **x**, **y** and **z**. Use a pair of compasses to draw arcs **a** and **b**, and then use the points where they intersect the arms of the angle as centres for drawing arcs with a smaller radius to intersect at **c**. A line joining **x** to **c** will bisect the angle.

6 BISECTING AN ANGLE: WORKSHOP METHOD

Imagine you are confronted with a large sheet of MDF or of chipboard, and that you have to bisect one of the corners as shown: the angle

6 BISECTING AN ANGLE: WORKSHOP METHOD

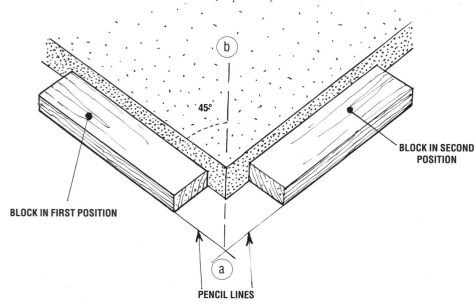

BLOCK IN SECOND POSITION

BLOCK IN FIRST POSITION

PENCIL LINES

⑦ DRAWING AN OCTAGON

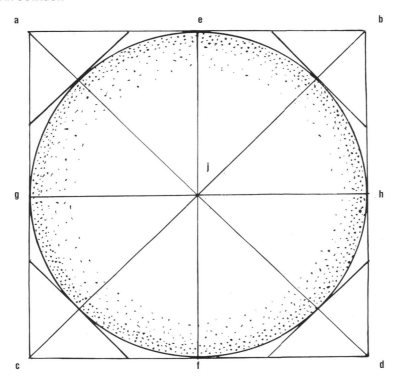

illustrated is a right angle, but the method works for an angle of any size.

You will need a block of wood of any convenient thickness, width or length, and its sides must be exactly parallel. Butt the block alongside the edge of the sheet and draw a pencil line along its free edge. Then repeat the process along one other edge of the sheet and draw another line. Extend the lines if necessary until they intersect at **a** and then draw another line from **a** through the corner and extend it as necessary to **b**. The line **ab** will bisect the angle.

7 DRAWING AN OCTAGON IN A SQUARE

Start by drawing the square **abcd** as shown and then mark in the diagonals **ad** and **bc**. Now draw in the vertical and horizontal lines **ef** and **gh**, and use the point **j** where the lines cross as the centre from which to draw the circle.

At each point where a radiating line (radius) cuts the circle, draw a line at right angles to it.

Following this procedure all around the circle will produce an octagon.

8 SQUARING MARKER FOR AN OCTAGON

9 MARKING GAUGE FOR AN OCTAGON

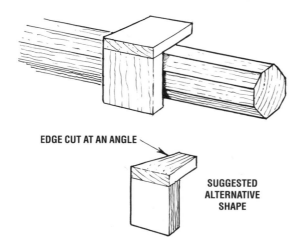

EDGE CUT AT AN ANGLE

SUGGESTED
ALTERNATIVE
SHAPE

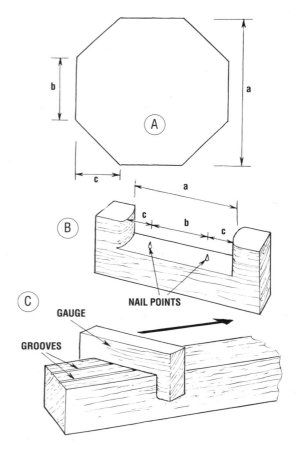

NAIL POINTS

GAUGE

GROOVES

8 SQUARING MARKS AROUND AN OCTAGON

The device shown here makes the job much easier than using a try square, which has a strong tendency to slide about because of the small surface it has to bear against. The home-made marker is thick enough to solve the problem.

9 MARKING OUT AN OCTAGON ON A STRAIGHT OR TAPERED WORKPIECE

This can be a tricky job whether the workpiece has parallel or tapered sides, and anything which makes marking out quick and easy – as this gauge does – is to be welcomed.

First, draw out the octagon to match the thickest part of the workpiece, as shown in **fig A**. From this you can see that there are three significant dimensions, namely **a**, **b** and **c**.

Next, prepare the block for the gauge from a piece of scrap wood so that you can hold it comfortably – the points shown in **fig B** are intended as a guide only and should be adjusted as appropriate. Now cut out the opening to suit the job and position the nails, allowing the points to protrude and so mark the lines.

To use the gauge, hold it firmly across the workpiece and run it back and forth to mask grooves as shown in **fig C**. The inner edges of the opening should be rounded off as shown in **fig B** to make this easier.

You can also use the gauge to mark off the centre lines for flutes or reeds by tapping in another nail between the first two, and by filing the ends of the nails to the correct profile you could actually scratch in the lines.

10 MODIFIED MARKING GAUGE

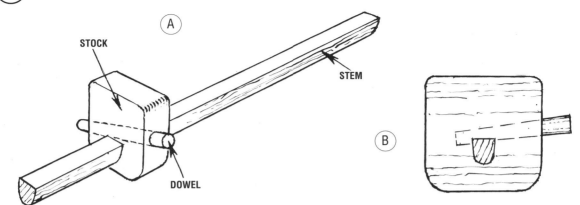

10 MODIFIED MARKING GAUGE

Ordinary gauges have a screw which is tightened on the stem to hold the stock in the required position, but in this design the screw is replaced by a piece of dowel which fits into a slanting hole drilled through the stock, as shown in **fig A**. The dowel is tapered and has a notch worked on the end plus a short flat surface which bears on the stem of the gauge, the notch ensuring that the dowel-wedge cannot fall out, as shown in **fig B**. The wedge is pushed forward with the thumb of the hand holding the stock, which is more convenient than having to turn a screw.

11 MULTI-ANGLE GAUGE

Ordinary sliding bevels can certainly be used to transfer any angle from one workpiece to another, but as the longest blade is rarely longer than 265mm (10½in) they can be too small for large work. This gauge can have as long a blade as you are likely to need and if made from 19mm (¾in) hardwood it should stay accurate for years.

Cut out a piece about 140 x 100mm (5½ x 4in) and then mark the hole for the pivot bolt. Using this as the centre, describe a semicircle,

11 MULTI-ANGLE GAUGE

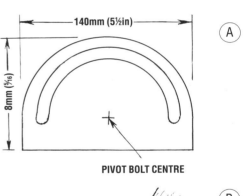

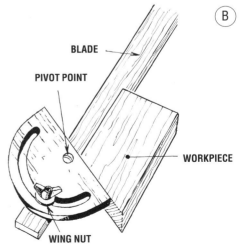

followed by two more which mark the curved slot shown in **fig A**. **Fig B** shows how the stock and the blade are bolted together, and how a bolt and wing nut positioned through the slot (which can be jigsawn or routed out) enables you to adjust the blade to a wide range of different angles.

12 MARKING OUT A SHALLOW CURVE WITH NO CENTRE

For this technique you will need two long, thin wooden strips. Begin by drawing a long straight line from **a** to **b**, with a shorter vertical line at its centre as shown in **fig A**: point **c** is located on this shorter line where the degree of curve is greatest.

Next, tap in nails at **a** and **b**, but leave them protruding slightly so that the strips can be run against them. At point **c**, nail the strips together tightly as shown in **fig B**; then hold a pencil at the intersection, and it will draw in the curve as they are moved back and forth against the nails, as shown in **fig C**.

13 GRADED DRAWER FRONTS

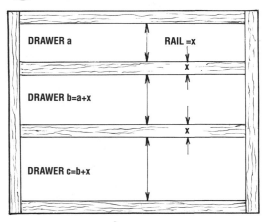

13 DRAWER FRONT DEPTHS

Where a design features several drawers one above the other, as in a chest of drawers, it will appear top-heavy if all the drawer fronts are the same depth.

The figure shows a suggested method of grading the drawer fronts by making each one the same depth as the one above plus the thickness of the dividing rail (**x**).

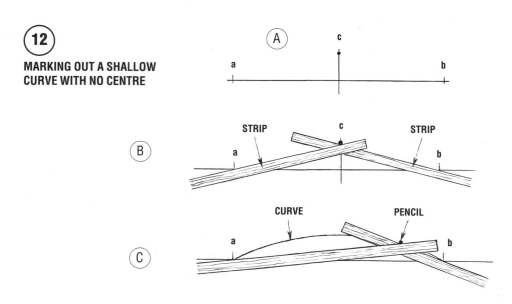

12

MARKING OUT A SHALLOW CURVE WITH NO CENTRE

14 PLOTTING THE PIVOT POINT FOR A SWIVELLING TABLE TOP

The formula for this is as follows: in the figure, dimension **y** equals half the length of side **a**, minus one-quarter of the length of **b**, and dimension **x** equals half the length of **a**, minus dimension **y**.

15 THE GOLDEN RULE

Also called the Golden Rectangle, the Golden Mean or the Divine Proportion, this formula was known to the ancient Egyptians and is considered by many eminent designers to give a perfectly proportioned rectangle.

The verbal expression of the formula is that the proportion of three dimensions is such that the first dimension is to the second as the second is to the whole (or the sum) of the two dimensions. This may be difficult to visualize and so is illustrated here both as a line divided into the proportions and as a rectangle. To sum up, a rectangle with two sides each one unit long and the other two sides each 1.618 units long is in perfect proportion.

Because the units are in proportion to each other in the ratio of 1.618:1, if you multiply both sides by, say, five, the result is a ratio of 8.090:5 which, as a rule of thumb for workshop use, we can regard as 8:5. Therefore, rectangles of 8 x 5cm, 8 x 5in or 8 x 5m (from which you will understand that the unit itself is irrelevant) will all be in perfect proportion.

14 PIVOT POINT FOR A SWIVELLING TABLE TOP

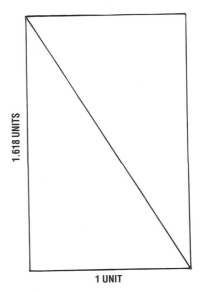

15 THE GOLDEN RULE

16 RIGHT-ANGLED TRIANGLE

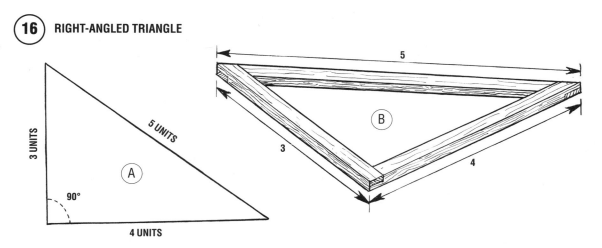

16 RIGHT-ANGLED TRIANGLE

This kind of triangle has several characteristics, one of the most important from our point of view being that the sum of the squares on its two shorter sides (the base and the perpendicular) is always equal to the square on its longest side (the hypoteneuse).

Fig A shows that this holds good for a right-angled triangle with sides of 3, 4 and 5 units – and the units can be centimetres, inches, metres, yards, kilometres, miles or anything else you like. The ancient Egyptians knew about this characteristic and we can borrow one of their tools: the right-angled set-square shown in

fig B, which is particularly useful outdoors where dimensions are likely to be larger than in the workshop.

17 REDUCING OR ENLARGING MOULDINGS FROM A SAMPLE

To begin this procedure, draw your sample moulding and mark it **abc** as shown. As a working example, let's assume that the reduced and enlarged mouldings to match it need to be 25mm (1in) and 75mm (3in) deep respectively.

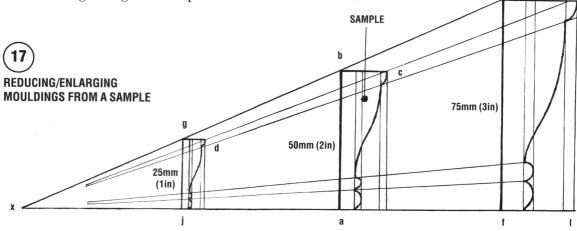

Through **a** draw a horizontal line **xl** of any convenient length as a base line, and through **b** draw the line **xk**, again of any convenient length. Draw in the verticals **jg** and **fk**, making them 25mm (1in) and 75mm (3in) long respectively. Next, from **g** and **k** draw horizontal lines parallel to the base line **xl**. From **x** draw a line to **c**, extending it to cut the horizontal line from **k** at **e**: this will give the widest points **gd** and **ke** of the required mouldings.

Draw ordinates (reference lines) from **x** through any suitable reference points on the sample moulding to plot the profiles on the required mouldings.

18 MARKING AND CUTTING OUT A TAPERED SPIRAL

When you have turned the tapered column on which a spiral twist is to be worked, the first step is to divide its overall length into equal parts, as shown in **fig A**.

Measuring the diameter at the centre of the column with calipers and dividing it into the length normally gives an acceptable result, but you can vary the proportions – thus a larger

18 **MARKING OUT A TAPERED SPIRAL**

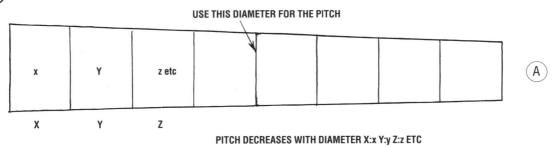

USE THIS DIAMETER FOR THE PITCH

x   Y   z etc

X   Y   Z

A

PITCH DECREASES WITH DIAMETER X:x Y:y Z:z ETC

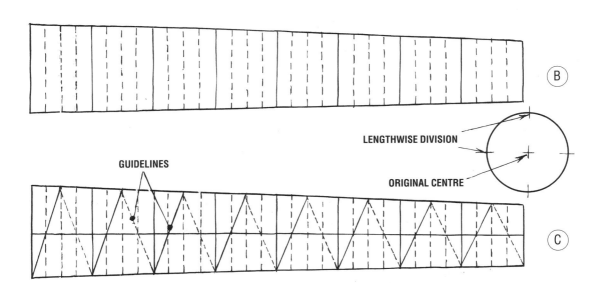

B

LENGTHWISE DIVISION

ORIGINAL CENTRE

GUIDELINES

C

diameter will yield a long, slow twist and, conversely, a smaller diameter a short, quicker one. Obviously, the diameter will rarely divide into the length exactly and a pair of dividers may be needed to achieve the precise measurement.

Having done this, divide each section you have just marked into four as shown in **fig B** and then divide the column lengthwise, again into four, as shown in **fig C**. To do this, mark two diameters at right angles to each other at both ends (you can probably use your original centring marks as a guide) and join the points where they touch the circumference along the column length.

The next step is to join the points where the lines intersect, and one of the best ways to do this is by winding a strip of transparent adhesive tape around the column. Finally, pencil along the outside edges of the tape. When this is removed, the marking out is complete.

All this work can be done with the column still in the lathe (with the power switched off), and this includes actually shaping the twist. You can carry out the shaping with a mallet and carving gouges, but the easiest way is to stick two thin strips of wood to the blade of your tenon saw with double-sided adhesive tape, one on each side, to act as depth guides, and then saw lightly along the spiral lines. Use a gouge to make a trench between the sawcuts, and follow this with a round surform rasp, files and glasspaper to finish off.

19 PLOTTING A SCROLL

To begin this procedure, first determine the overall width of the scroll **ab** and divide it into eight equal parts; then draw in **ac** so that it is the same length as one division. Join **c** to **b**. Using point 4 as a centre, with a pair of compasses draw an arc which just touches the line **cb** as a tangent and meets line **ab** at a new point **d**. From **d** draw a line downwards at right angles to the line **ab**, and another line from **c** parallel to **ab**.

Now you can start to draw the outline of the scroll using a succession of points as centres. Start with point **d** as a centre and use your compasses to draw the arc **bf**: point **f** is where the arc meets the extension of the line **de**. Next, use point **e** as the centre for drawing the arc **fc**. From **f** draw a line to the line **bc** which meets it at a right angle at point **g**; then draw another line from **d** through **g** to meet the line **ce**.

Referring now to the enlarged drawing, you will see that you can plot the figure described by the points **e**, **h**, **j**, **k** and **l**. Point **h** is the next

⑲ PLOTTING A SCROLL

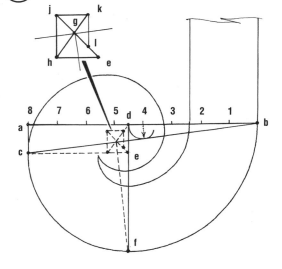

centre from which to draw an arc; the following centre is point **k** and the last one **l**. Arcs drawn from these points will complete the outer line of the scroll, and the inner line can be drawn parallel to it.

20 THREE WAYS TO DRAW AN ELLIPSE

The first method is the 'pins and string' technique, shown in **fig A**. Draw the two axes which are the greatest length and greatest breadth, shown as **ab** and **cd**, with **e** as the centre point where they intersect at right angles. From **c**, setting your compasses with **a** to **e** as radius, draw two arcs to cut **ab** at **g** and **f** and drive a nail or pin partway home at each point. Tie a piece of string into a loop around the pins and with a pencil inside the loop start drawing the ellipse, keeping the string taut at all times.

At **x**, you will see that a 'tangent' and a 'normal' have been introduced. These are particularly useful when, for instance, aligning the face of a leg on an elliptical coffee table, a job which would otherwise have to be done by eye. Let us suppose that **x** is where you want to position the leg: join both **f** and **g** to **x** and bisect the angle thus formed – the bisecting line is the normal and the tangent is drawn at right angles to it.

20 METHODS FOR DRAWING AN ELLIPSE

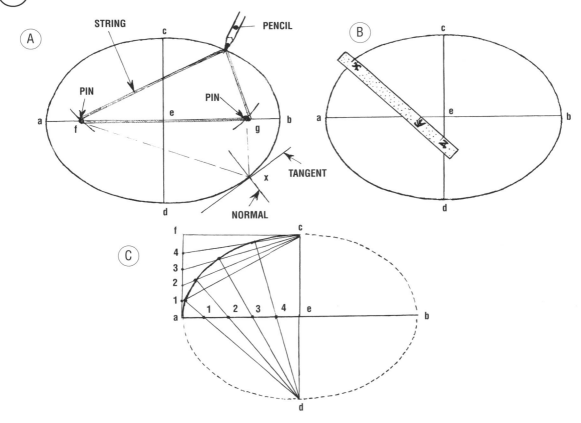

The second way to draw an ellipse is the 'trammel' method, shown in **fig B**. Draw the axes **ab** and **cd** to intersect at **e** as described for the previous method. Next, cut a strip of thin card and mark off **xz** equal to **ae** and **xy** equal to **ce**, then place the strip of card (the trammel) on the drawing so that **z** is on the shorter axis and **y** is on the longer one, as shown. Mark a point at **x** which will be found to be on the outline of the ellipse, then move the trammel round, keeping **y** and **z** on the axes, and make another mark at **x**. Carry on doing this until you have enough marks to draw the ellipse freehand.

The third way is the 'intersecting lines' method, shown in **fig C**. Draw the axes **ab** and **cd** as before, and then on **ae** draw a rectangle **aecf**. Divide **ae** and **af** into the same

number of convenient parts and draw lines from **d** through the points on **ae** and from the points on **af** to **c**. Each intersection of these lines will be a point on the ellipse and they can be joined freehand. You can repeat the process for the other three sections, or trace off the outline and transfer it to them using carbon paper.

21 SETTING OUT A HIPPED DESIGN

This type of design is sometimes used for the lids of jewellery or trinket boxes, and also for the roofs of dolls' houses. The difficulty is that you are dealing with inclined planes which meet at compound angles; **figs A** and **B** therefore show how the problem can be dealt with geometrically.

Start by drawing half the side elevation, marking in the line **AE**, then draw the end

21 SETTING OUT A HIPPED DESIGN

SIDE ELEVATION

END ELEVATION

B or A   D or C

A

HIPPED TOP

B

PLAN

elevation **BDF** and the plan **ABCD**, all of which are shown in **fig A**. Now draw in the line **ac** parallel to **AC**, the distance **G** between them being the height of the end elevation. Similarly, draw **a'b'** parallel to **AB** at a distance equal to **H** in the side elevation. The lengths **a'c'** and **b'd'** are arrived at by extending **AC** and **BD** respectively, and the drawing then becomes a plane (flattened) version of the hipped top design shown in **fig B**.

22 DOVETAIL MARKING

Traditionally there are three different angles of slope for the sides of dovetails, namely 1 in 6, 1 in 7 or 1 in 8. The narrower the angle, the more suitable it is deemed to be for prime hardwoods, while the greater angle given by a slope of 1 in 6 can be employed for softwoods. Today,

however, the 1 in 7 slope is the one used by most woodworkers, especially as the kind of dovetail used is, more often than not, determined by the many guides and jigs which allow dovetails to be cut by power routers.

The two templates shown in **figs A** and **B** are helpful if you are cutting dovetails by hand, and both can be made from acrylic sheet. The one shown in **fig A** consists of a piece of the sheet which is set into a groove in a wooden block and held by ordinary woodscrews; it gives a 1 in 7 angle. The advantage of this design becomes apparent when you need to mark a dovetail slope which is set in from the edge by such a small amount that the template shown in **fig B** could not be held in place. This second template can also be made from acrylic sheet and is suitable for marking out a row of dovetails.

22 **DOVETAIL TEMPLATES**

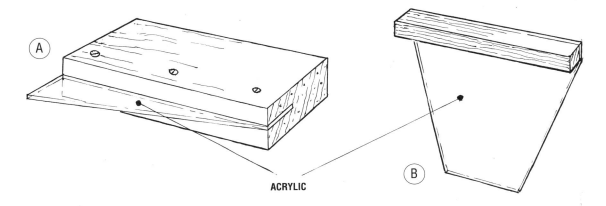

Ⓐ

Ⓑ

ACRYLIC

23 DIVIDING RANDOM WIDTHS INTO EQUAL PARTS

Any width of board can be divided by placing a rule across at an angle so that the distance between any two divisions on it can be divided into equal parts; see **fig 23**.

24 PINCH ROD

This device can be used to measure inside dimensions – for example, inside a box or even between two walls. Normally, pinch rods are made so that both rods move against each other, but this type of arrangement can be unwieldy as you need to use both hands.

In the design shown in **fig 24**, one rod is glued permanently into a hole in the upper part of the block, while the other slides freely through a hole drilled in the bottom part. The rods can be 12mm (½in) dowel with the ends sharpened to a chisel shape: suggested sizes are given for the fixed rod and the block, while the sliding rod can be of any length to suit the job.

(23) DIVIDING RANDOM WIDTHS INTO EQUAL PARTS

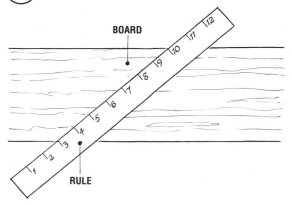

BOARD

RULE

As the amount of adjustment is governed by the length of the block, it is a good idea to have two or three of varying lengths to cover jobs of different sizes.

The diameter of the dowels here has been chosen so that you can tighten a hose clip of the same size at the required point and then move the pinch rods about without losing the measurement.

(24) PINCH ROD

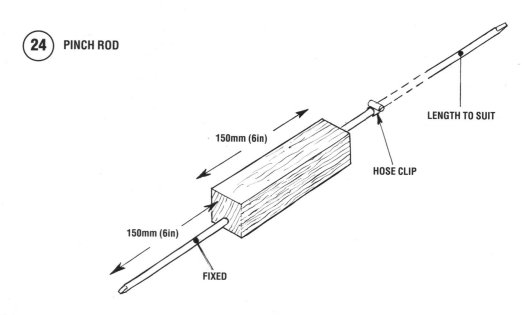

150mm (6in)

LENGTH TO SUIT

HOSE CLIP

150mm (6in)

FIXED

25 ADJUSTABLE SQUARE

This is a large square very suitable for joinery work and invaluable for measuring the angles of room corners, which are seldom exact right angles.

Figs A and **B** show the construction, which comprises three parts: the fixed arm, the movable arm and the diagonal strut. The sizes given below are suggestions only, and you can alter them to suit your purposes.

Make the fixed arm from three laminations glued together, but with a slot left at one end in which the movable arm is inserted. The laminations could be three laths glued together, each 45 x 12mm (1¾ x ½in), and the same size could be used for the other parts.

Note that the diagonal strut is stepped up to allow for the difference in levels. Drill holes, centrally in the fixed arm, and at one end of the diagonal strut, to accept a 6mm (¼in) bolt with a washer and wing nut; and then drill holes to take two more similar wing nuts: at the other end of the diagonal strut, and also at the ends of the movable and fixed arms (see **fig A**).

Assemble the parts and cut a slot in the moveable arm for the wing nut and bolt to slide in, so that when the arms are at exactly 90 degrees the bolt lies in the centre of the slot; it is a good idea to mark the position of the strut on the movable arm so that you can use the square as a normal right-angled one.

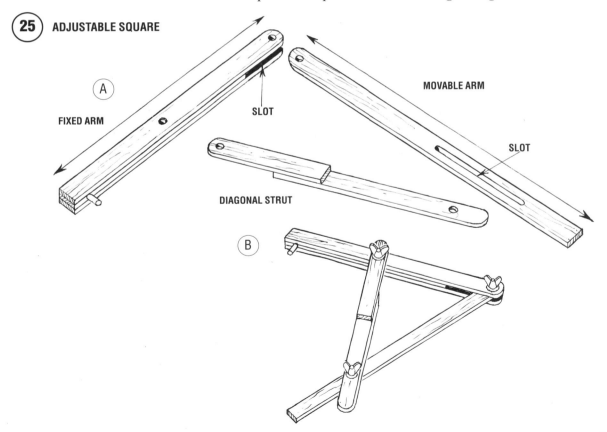

25 ADJUSTABLE SQUARE

A

FIXED ARM

SLOT

MOVABLE ARM

SLOT

DIAGONAL STRUT

B

26 MARKING OUT CURVES

The essential component for this technique is a long, thin lath which is free from knots, splits or cross-grain and is the same thickness throughout its length. A hardwood such as beech is best, and although strips of ply or hardboard may look tempting they do not give such a regular, sweet curve.

You will need to mark out the two end points and the centre point on the workpiece, in order to ascertain the shape of the curve. The simplest method is shown in **fig A** and relies on the power of twisted string to pull the lath into a curve. Needless to say, the string loop must be firmly secured at each end; the string is twisted by means of a suitable piece of scrap wood, which is inserted in the middle of the loop and then turned over and over. Once curved, the ends can be cramped to the workpiece and the curve drawn in.

A more sophisticated technique is shown in **fig B**. This is more rigid and gives a curve that is consistent throughout its length. The lath is centred on a small block which has a rounded nose and is cramped in place, then the ends of the lath are pulled back to their respective marks and are also cramped. The curve can then be drawn in.

26 **MARKING OUT CURVES**

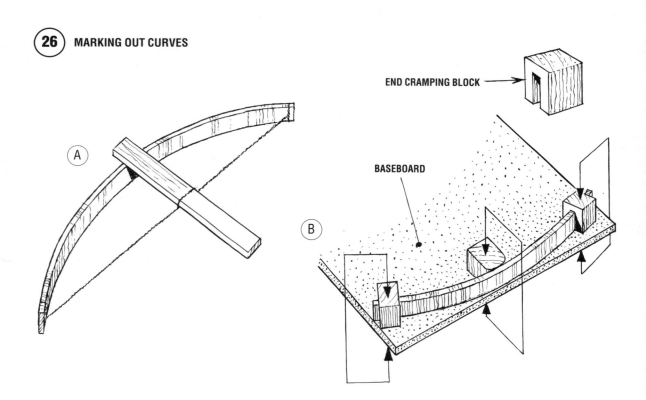

END CRAMPING BLOCK

BASEBOARD

27 SCRIBING TEMPLATE FOR CURVES

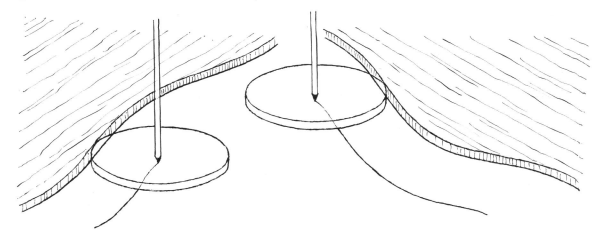

27 SCRIBING TEMPLATE FOR CURVES

This template consists of a disc of hardboard, thin ply or acrylic sheet which can be turned on the lathe or sawn out by means of a jigsaw or a padsaw (depending on the material) and then trued up on a disc sander, as described on page 46.

Drill a small hole at the exact centre and insert a ballpoint pen or a marking awl so that the disc will revolve freely around it. The radius of the disc must, of course, equal the distance from the pattern of the new line to be marked. In use, the disc simply runs along the edge of the pattern and can be used on interior or exterior curves.

28 DEPTH GAUGE

This device consists of a blunt-pointed dowel which is a sliding fit in a block and is held in position with a dowel-wedge, as shown.

The block need only be about 75mm (3in) long for normal work such as measuring the depths of mortises or the holes for dowels, but

28 DEPTH GAUGE

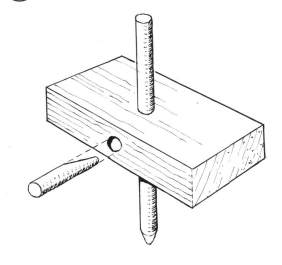

if you want to use it to check the depth of bowls that are being turned it will need to be considerably longer.

(29) GRASSHOPPER GAUGE

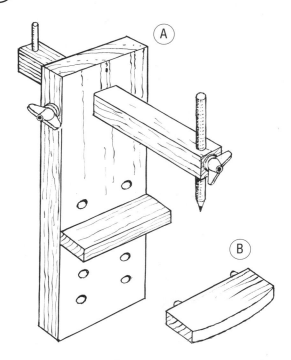

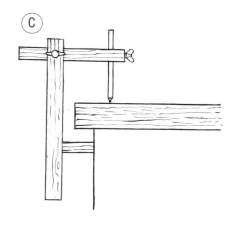

29 GRASSHOPPER GAUGE

This is the gauge traditionally used in circumstances such as the one shown in **fig C**, where a line is being marked around an overhanging table top.

The construction is shown in **fig A** and the sizes will be determined by the kind of work you are doing. The stem slides snugly through a hole in the fence and can have the conventional point at one end and a hole for a pencil at the other. Both fixings – the one which tightens on the fence as well as the one that holds the pencil – consist of wing nuts and bolts which thread through tee-nuts, or hexagonal nuts glued in place with an epoxy resin adhesive.

The smaller horizontal fence is fitted with dowels which must be a tight fit into the holes drilled for them. An alternative fence for curved work is shown in **fig B**, and if neither of the smaller fences is fitted the gauge can be used on deep work.

Chapter 9

FITTINGS AND HARDWARE

noquote K nock-down (KD) fittings were developed originally to allow manufacturers to transport furniture economically in a pack-flat form. Today, when it is difficult to make a cabinet without using man-made boards, such as chipboard or MDF, they have become indispensable, as it is sometimes difficult to fasten these materials by conventional methods. The ones most likely to be useful to the home woodworker are described in this chapter, which also covers a selection of hinges and other hardware.

KNOCK-DOWN FITTINGS

1 CHIPBOARD FASTENERS

It is notoriously tricky to insert woodscrews into the edges of man-made boards as they tend to create bulges, and all too often the fixing is so weak that they can be pulled out with thumb and finger.

Chipboard fasteners are certain to give a really firm fixing without bulging. They are made from nylon, threaded internally, and are available in several lengths: you must, however, use the recommended gauge of screw.

1 CHIPBOARD FASTENER

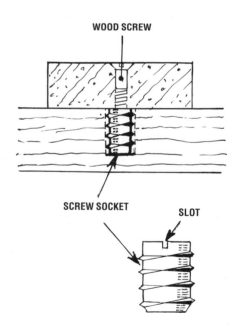

WOOD SCREW

SCREW SOCKET

SLOT

2 BLOC-JOINT FITTING

Also called 'assembly blocks', these are made from hard plastic. One half has two pegs which locate into holes on the other half, plus a machine screw which ensures that two panels meeting in a butt joint will be held accurately at right angles, as shown.

There is a smaller pattern called a 'Modesty' bloc which is less obtrusive and this can be utilized for light work. The name derives from the original use of the blocks, which was to fix a 'modesty' panel in the kneehole of a pedestal desk so that the legs of the young lady at the desk could not be seen.

2 BLOC-JOINT FITTING

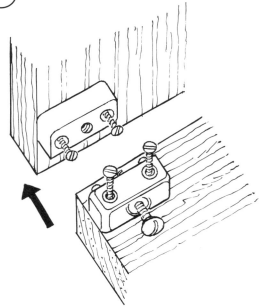

3 TAPER CONNECTOR

This fitting is in two parts, both made from heavy-gauge steel, consisting of a wedge-shaped section which slides downwards into a matching channel as shown. It is intended for use with heavy frameworks and also for hanging wall cabinets, when the channel acting as a socket is fixed to the wall.

3 TAPER CONNECTOR

4 CONNECTING SCREW

Also called an 'inter-screw', this is handy for connecting cabinets side by side and can be used where the combined thicknesses of the panels is between 30mm and 39mm (1¼in and 1¾in). The figure shows the way in which the screws are fitted.

4 CONNECTING SCREW

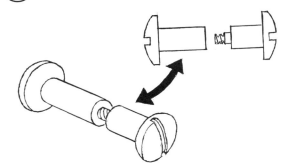

(5) PANEL CONNECTOR

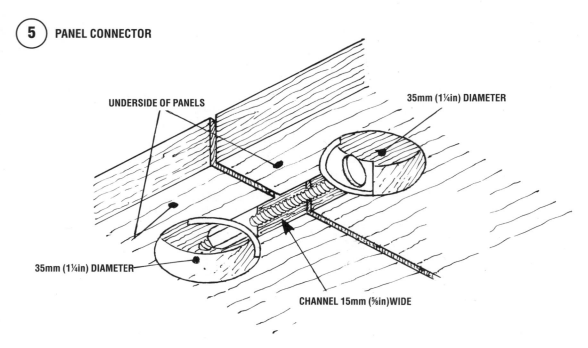

UNDERSIDE OF PANELS

35mm (1¼in) DIAMETER

35mm (1¼in) DIAMETER

CHANNEL 15mm (⅝in) WIDE

5 PANEL CONNECTOR

Also called a 'worktop clamp', this connector is particularly useful when panels or worktops have to be jointed end to end, as shown. The two 35mm (1¼in) diameter holes are connected by a 15mm (⅝in) wide channel, into which the threaded bolt is inserted. Tightening the hexagonal nut draws the panels together.

6 ASSEMBLY FITTING

This fitting consists of two components as shown in **fig A**. Fitting consists of boring two 25mm (1in) diameter holes, one in each of the boards to be joined – the special boring bit for doing this is shown in **fig B**. Each component threads into its appropriate hole and the peg is inserted into the cavity; the screw is given half a turn and moves a cam, which engages into the peg and locks the joint, as shown in **fig C**.

(6) ASSEMBLY FITTING

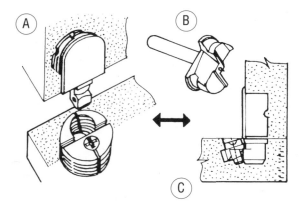

7 MORTISE EDGE-TO-EDGE FITTING

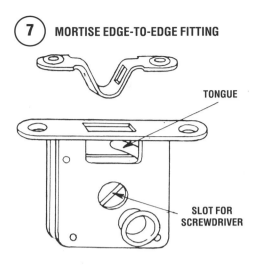

TONGUE

SLOT FOR
SCREWDRIVER

9 CABINET HANGER

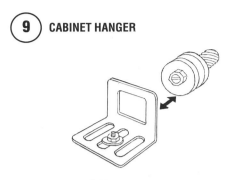

9 CABINET HANGER

Designed to allow considerable latitude when fixing a cabinet to a wall, this fitting consists of a bracket which is bolted to the cupboard panel and then hung on to a circular cam which is screwed to the wall. There is an allowance of up to 12mm (½in) for movement sideways and up to 10mm (⅜in) in height. The hanger can be used in a similar fashion on the cabinet underside, which is particularly valuable when it has to be hung flush with the ceiling.

7 MORTISE EDGE-TO-EDGE FITTING

As its name implies, this fitting joins panels edge to edge, using a mortise made in each edge – a deep one for the body and a shallower one for the catch. Turning a screwdriver in the slot moves a tongue, which engages in slots in the catch.

8 'FIX' CAM FITTING

This fitting is useful for cabinet construction, particularly when chipboard is involved; the minimum thickness of the parts to be joined must be 13mm (½in). When the cam is tightened by turning a screwdriver in the slot, it bears on the bolt and takes up any slackness between the parts. Also supplied is a plastic cap for covering the fitting.

10 INTERLOCKING BED FITTING

An interlocking fitting made from steel is simple to fit, as one part slots over the other to make a strong fitting that can be taken apart easily when necessary.

10 INTERLOCKING BED FITTING

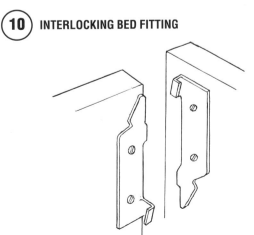

8 'FIX' CAM FITTING

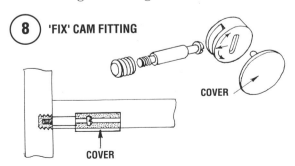

COVER

COVER

HINGES

1 **SINGLE CRANKED CABINET HINGE**

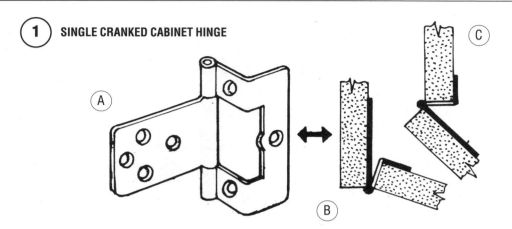

1 SINGLE CRANKED CABINET HINGE

Using this hinge, doors can be hinged either flush or lay-on, and in both cases extra support is given to the door by the two screwed fixings – one in the end and the other to the inside face. No recessing is required, and only the knuckle shows when the door is closed. The minimum thickness required is 16mm (⅝in).

The hinge is shown in **fig A**. **Fig B** shows it with the door hinged flush, while in **fig C** it is lay-on. It could also be used on the flap of the locker-type cupboard which is sometimes found on the top of a wardrobe.

2 'SEPA' HINGE

This was one of the first concealed cabinet hinges and is still one of the best. It is completely hidden when the door is closed, yet allows it to open to a full 180 degrees and, unlike some other designs, requires no special hole-boring bit. It can be used for lay-on or flush doors, flaps or concertina-type panels.

You will need to recess the hinge into the

edge of the door and the side by 7mm (⁷⁄₁₆in), and it is then fastened by four countersunk-head wood screws in each plate. Note that the minimum thickness of board that can be used is 19mm (¾in).

2 **'SEPA' HINGE**

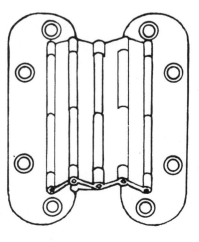

3 CONCEALED CABINET HINGES

Concealed hinges as shown in **fig A** have been developed for use with furniture constructed from man-made boards, many of which are not capable of holding traditional cabinet hinges close to their edges or in end grain. They have a number of desirable characteristics:

- The hinges have some built-in adjustments so as to take up any small inaccuracies in construction.
- Adjoining doors can be opened without fouling one another, and the door on an end cabinet which is located against a wall can be opened fully.
- There are four choices of opening angle: 100, 110, 125 and 170 degrees.
- Most of the hinges can be purchased either sprung or unsprung, the only difference being that with the sprung model the door will stay closed without the need for a retaining catch.

- The hinge is completely hidden when the door is closed.
- A range of mini-hinges is available, these simply being smaller versions of the standard models, as shown in **fig B**.

For standard sizes you will need a 35mm diameter hinge-sinker, and for mini-hinges a 26mm one. This is a special boring tool which must be used to make an accurate, flat-bottomed hole for the barrel of the hinge.

4 FLUSH-FITTING FLAP HINGE

With this type of hinge, the hinge body is fitted by drilling a 35mm diameter hole, which is the only size available, in the side of the cabinet and another 30mm in diameter for the catch in the door or lid; the centres for both holes must be 12.5mm (½in) away from the edges. When the hinge has been fitted, you can adjust it sideways or to be flush, or to stand slightly proud.

3   **CONCEALED CABINET HINGES**

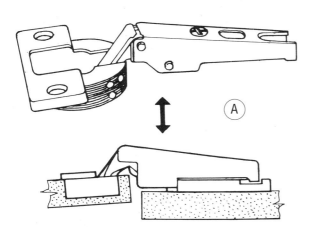

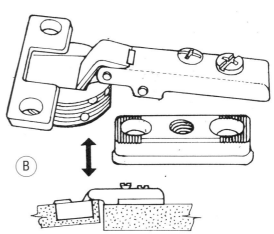

4 **FLUSH-FITTING FLAP HINGE**

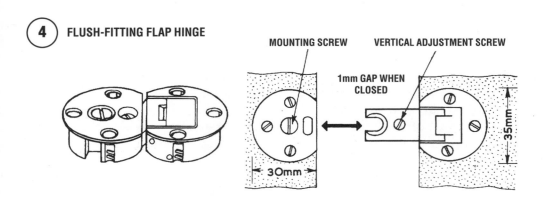

MOUNTING SCREW

VERTICAL ADJUSTMENT SCREW

1mm GAP WHEN
CLOSED

30mm

35mm

MISCELLANEOUS HARDWARE

1 **REPAIR PLATES**

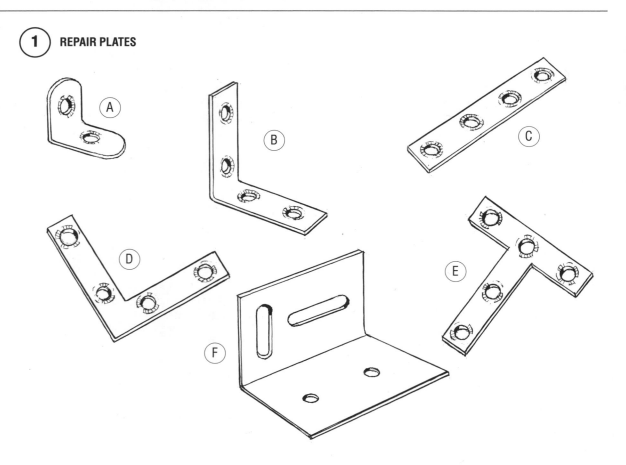

2 SLIDING DRAWER RUNNER

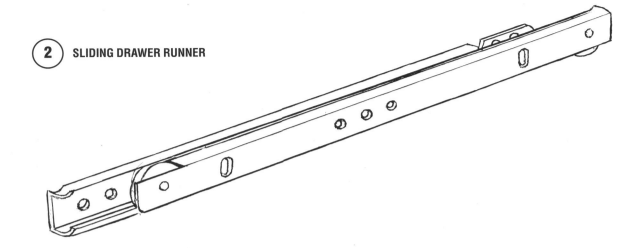

1 REPAIR PLATES

The repair plates shown here are: an angle brace (**fig A**); a corner brace (**fig B**); a mending plate (**fig C**); a right-angled plate (**fig D**); a tee plate (**fig E**); and a shrinkage plate (**fig F**). The latter allows for any movement of adjacent wooden parts, as the screws which are inserted through the slots are not driven home tightly.

2 SLIDING DRAWER RUNNER

The runner shown here is normally used for sliding drawers. Each runner includes a trapped roller which eliminates any sideways movement. The runners are supplied in handed pairs, and can be side- or bottom-fixing.

3 MIRROR PIVOTS

Mirror pivots are supplied in handed pairs and are used to fix mirrors so that they can be swivelled between pillars. Part **A** is screwed to the pillar while part **B** is fastened to the edge of the mirror. The lug on **B** swivels and can be dropped into the tapered flanges on **A**.

3 MIRROR PIVOTS

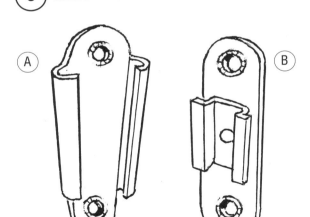

TECHNICAL TERMS EXPLAINED

Air-seasoned Description of timber that has been allowed to season naturally, protected from rain. A rule of thumb is that hardwoods take approximately one year to dry for every 25mm (1in) of thickness.

Apron 'Apron-piece' generally refers to the shaped parts often fitted under the middle drawer of a knee hole writing or dressing table. An 'apron board' is also the vertical wide board along the front of a workbench.

Architrave Moulded surround of a door or of a window.

Arris Actual edge between two surfaces meeting at an angle and usually referred to simply as the 'edge'.

Astragal Combined bead and fillet moulding used on the closing edges of double doors. In narrow widths it is employed in the barred doors of bookcases, display cabinets etc.

Back flaps Any hinge on which the leaves have more than one row of holes.

Bail handle Half-loop metal pull handle, where the handle part is suspended from a bolt at each end.

Bare Term used in imperial sizes when measuring and meaning 'slightly less than'. Thus 'one inch bare' is approximately $\frac{1}{32}$in less than 1in.

Bench dog Metal or wood sprung pegs, usually about 25mm (1in) square, which fit into a line of holes along the top of a workbench and form end stops when used in conjunction with a tail vice.

Bevel Edge which comprises two surfaces meeting at any angle other than a right angle.

Bleed-through Unwanted penetration of an adhesive or a polish stain through a veneer or other thin wood.

Blind Description applied to a tenon or pierced work which does not fully penetrate the wood.

Bole Main trunk of a tree.

Bolection moulding Moulding rebated along one edge so that it will fit over a framework.

Book matching Term used in veneering to describe how two consecutive leaves of veneer are laid side by side but with one turned the other way up so that the grain of both is exactly matched. Also called 'halved pattern'.

Burr (in wood) Highly figured veneer cut across the wart-like excrescence which sometimes grows at the base of a tree. It is caused by a number of buds clustered together that fail to develop fully because of lack of nourishment.

Butt That part of a tree from the ground to the point where the main branches begin.

Cambium Cells which lie just beneath the bark of a tree and are responsible for transmitting sap.

Canted Inclined or arranged at an angle, as in a bevel (see above).

Carcase Skeletal framework of a piece of cabinet furniture such as a bookcase, chest of drawers, wardrobe etc.

Card-cut Describes fretted or lattice work which is 'blind' (see above).

Case hardening Applies to wood which, through faulty seasoning, has been dried too quickly on the outside, thereby causing stresses which may not be apparent until the wood is further developed.

Casting Twisting or warping of a board caused either by faulty seasoning or by being veneered on one side only.

Chamfer Similar to a bevel (see above), but not necessarily occupying the whole thickness of the wood as a bevel does. It is also 'stopped' (allowed to run out) at each end.

Check Split along the length of a board, usually across the annual rings.

Cheeks Flat sides of a tenon.

Clamp Piece of wood fixed across the end of a table top which is made up of strips glued together side by side. The top is fixed into the clamp by an elongated mortise and tenon joint.

Cleat Piece of wood which acts as a support for a shelf, resists thrust or acts as a temporary cramp.

Clenching Bending over the point of a nail after it has passed through the wood so that it forms a kind of rivet.

Counter-boring Method of recessing a screw head deep into the wood by boring a hole large enough to accept the screw head first, then making a smaller hole for the shank at the end of the first hole. It enables a shorter screw to be used than would otherwise be possible.

Dado Panelling fixed to the walls of a room to a height of about 1m (39in); also refers to a dado moulding fixed at the same height but without the panelling. In the USA, it describes a groove or trench cut across the grain.

De-nib To remove nibs (specks of dust, hairs etc) from a painted or polished surface by lightly papering it with fine grades of abrasive papers.

Dip-seat Chair seat frame which is curved to match curved seat rails.

Doaty Wood that shows an early stage of attack by fungi.

Domes of silence Alternative name for the 'glides' which are often fixed to the feet of chairs and tables to protect floor coverings.

Droxy Term describing the early stages of decomposition characterized by white or yellow streaks along the grain.

Dub To round and smooth off.

Edge mark Vee-shaped mark on the face edge (see below) of timber to confirm that it is straight and square with the face side, which has already been trued.

Escutcheon Metal plate or lining which is fixed around a keyhole in order to protect the surrounding wood.

Extenders Powdered substances which can be added to some resin adhesives to bulk them up and increase their spreading ability. Common examples are china clay, kaolin and rye flour.

Face edge Edge of a piece of wood which has been planed straight and true with the face side, which has been prepared as the 'show' side.

Fielded panel Used in a framework or a door, this has a wide chamfered rebate worked around its edges so that the centre stands proud.

Full Term meaning 'slightly more than'; its converse is 'bare' (see above).

Gallery Low wooden or metal railing, usually pierced or decorated, fixed around a table top or something similar to prevent objects from falling off.

Girth Measurement around a tree or log if the tree tapers; it is usually taken around the centre as an average.

Gliders Flat polished steel domes with projecting spikes which hold them to the feet of chairs and tables; to protect carpets. *See also* Domes of silence.

Green Term applied to unseasoned and recently felled timber which is full of moisture.

Groundwork *See* Substrate.

Hammer veneering Technique for laying small areas of veneer – particularly any which have difficult grain, as in a burr – by pressing them down with a special hammer used in a zigzag motion.

Haunch Step or notch left uncut on a tenon to make it less likely to twist.

Honeycombing Fault in timber usually caused by case hardening (see above), consisting of small splits that are only revealed when the timber is cut across.

Horn Extra piece of wood allowed on a rail so that a mortise can be cut at the end without the risk of its splitting.

Increment teeth Saw teeth which become progressively larger towards the handle.

In the round Refers to felled timber which has not been squared up or converted.

In the white Refers to woodwork which has not been finished by polishing, painting or varnishing, so that the wood is in its natural state.

Iron Alternative name, albeit rather old-fashioned, for the cutter of a hand plane.

Jointing Technique of gluing long strips of wood together side by side to form a wide panel. No other kind of fastening is used and the joint relies solely on the glue. Also called 'rubbed jointing' or 'slaped jointing'.

Kerf Cut made by any kind of saw.

Keying I Method of strengthening a joint, usually a mitre, by the insertion of small keys or tongues.

Keying II Toothing or roughing a surface to provide better adhesion for glue.

Kickback If work is introduced to a machine too quickly or if it is too large, the machine is likely to reject it and throw it back violently and dangerously.

Lagging Process used for building up shaped work such as coving, consisting of screwing narrow strips to the pre-shaped ribs.

Lapped joint Joint where the edge of one part is rebated so that it laps over and covers the edge of the other.

Ledge Batten fixed across an assembly of tongued and grooved boards to hold it together. Commonly used in the ledged and braced doors employed on sheds.

Lipping Narrow strips of good-quality wood which are fixed to the raw edges of chipboards, plywood and the like to cover them and give them a more attractive appearance.

Live knot Knot which is firmly fixed as opposed to one that is loose.

Lopers Strips which slide forward to support the flap of a bureau or the loose leaves on an extending table.

Mandrel Revolving spindle of a lathe or circular saw. On a lathe it is usually hollow to accept various patterns of chuck.

Matchboarding Another name for tongued and grooved boards.

Monopodium Table, usually with a circular top, which is supported on a single pillar or column.

Morse drills Similar to the twist drills used in woodwork, but intended for metalwork.

Mould Alternative name for a template used for marking out shapes in woodworking.

Muntins Divisions in a framed-up door or carcase.

Nicker Small triangular knife edge in a centre bit which cuts the circular path before the cutter removes the wood.

Nominal size Refers to the dimensions of timber which has been converted by sawing but has not been planed or otherwise machined.

Open grain Timber grain which shows large pores: also called 'coarse grain'.

Out of true Term applied to any frame, carcase or structure which is not square or is twisted.

Paper joint Butt joint which is glued with a piece of paper between the parts, so that the joint can be broken apart easily when work is finished. Widely used when making split turnings.

Parcel Term used loosely to describe a quantity of timber or veneer, regardless of its size, grain or species.

Patera Circular or elliptical ornament often carved in low relief or made in marquetry which is glued or pinned on furniture as pure decoration or to hide an ugly feature. Can also be in metal.

Peen, Pene, Pein All describe the tapered blade opposite the head on certain types of metalworking hammers.

Pegged joint Type of mortise and tenon joint in which a peg (or pegs) is driven through the walls of the mortise and the tenon inside in order to strengthen it.

Peripheral speed Speed at which any one point on a circular saw is moving as it revolves. It can be found by multiplying the diameter of the saw by the rpm, multiplying again by 3.14 (pi) and then dividing by 1,000.

Pilasters Long, thin strips of wood which are often fluted or reeded, fixed to the front corners of pieces such as sideboards, display cabinets, bookcases etc.

Pin knot Small knot which is less than 6mm (¼in) in diameter.

Points Saw teeth are measured in points at so many per 25mm (1in), including those at both ends.

Pot life Maximum time for which a mixed adhesive remains usable. *See also* Shelf life.

Pummel Parts left square on a turning, usually so that rails can be fitted into them.

Racking Side pressure, first in one direction and then the other, which causes a frame or a carcase to go out of square.

Reeds Series of beads alongside each other, often used as a decorative feature on a pilaster (see above) or around a turned column.

Rift sawn   Another term for quarter-sawn.

Ripping   Sawing lengthwise along the grain.

Rod   Piece of drawing card, plywood or white plastic-faced board on which are drawn the outlines and constructional details of a job in the style of a cross-section or elevation. They are drawn full size so that the actual parts of the job can be laid on them as a check. All details such as handles, mouldings, joints etc should be included, although they would not normally appear in the cross-section.

Rosin   Natural gum which is a by-product of the distillation of pure turpentine. It can be used to harden wax polishes or to make stopping.

Run out   Term applied to a moulding or chamfer which, instead of continuing through the whole length or finishing at a stop, gradually fades out to the surface.

Safe edges   Describes a file having edges free from teeth.

Sap stain   Result of a fungal attack which leaves a blue stain. The strength of the timber is not affected, however, and it can still be used if the colour is not a disadvantage.

Sash   Glazed door of a bookcase which is divided into symmetrical rectangular panes.

Screw box and tap   Device for cutting screw threads in wood. It consists of two parts: the box, which has a vee-shaped cutter that shapes the thread, and the tap, which is a tapered steel bit with teeth made in different sizes to cut the holes.

Scribing   Process of shaping a piece of wood so that it fits to the shape of another or, in the case of a mitred joint, shaping the profile of one piece to match that of the other.

Secret nailing   Process of raising a sliver of wood without detaching it completely and driving the nail in under it so that it can be glued back in place. The term also refers to fastening tongued and grooved boards by nailing through the tongues, which are subsequently covered.

Shelf life   Length of time a can of adhesive can be stored before going off. *See also* Pot life.

Shoot   To plane an edge square and true, either by hand or machine.

Shorts or short ends   Trade term describing odd lengths of timber under 2m (6ft approx.) long.

Show wood   On upholstered furniture, wooden parts which are left purposely un-upholstered.

Sinking   Shallow recess cut or routed out of the solid.

Slip feather   Loose tongue with the grain running diagonally instead of at right angles. This allows longer tongues to be made, as they are not likely to break across the grain.

Soffit   Underside of an arch or opening.

Solid, in the   Refers to any detail, such as a decoration, moulding or patera (see above) that is worked from the solid as distinct from being applied.

Spalt   Wood which is brittle as a result of decay or over-drying. It is usually a light brown colour.

Spiling   Method of reproducing a curved or odd shape when direct measurement is impossible. A projecting door post with a moulded face is a good example. First, a piece of cardboard or thick paper with a straight edge is butted against a wall, with a gap cut away around the projection. A pointed object such as a set-square is placed in various positions on the card with its point touching the projection and its outline is then pencilled in.

When the cardboard is transferred to the wood which is to be cut out, the set-square can be replaced on the outlines and its point marked on the wood, thus reproducing the shape.

Split turning Ornamental turning where the two halves of the blank are glued together with a piece of paper interposed, so that they can be separated easily after turning.

Springing Bending a piece of wood to shorten its length so that it can enter mortises which are already fixed at each end – a cross rail in a chair back is a good example.

Stiles Vertical rails of a framed-up door, comprising the hanging stile and the closing stile, and in the case of double doors, the meeting stiles.

Stretcher Rail stretching from leg to leg in the underframes of chairs, tables etc, to give extra strength and enhance the appearance.

Substrate Surface specially suited to or prepared for subsequent veneering or covering with plastic sheet. Also called 'groundwork'.

Tack Degree of adhesion between two glued surfaces before the glue has finally set or cured, so that it still allows some adjustment.

Tack rag Piece of lint-free rag that has been dipped in varnish diluted with turpentine substitute (white spirit) and then wrung out. It collects the dust instead of spreading it into the air.

Telegraphing Effect obtained when veneers have been laid on an unsuitable groundwork. It usually begins to show as a ripple or shadowy patches some time after the veneering.

Thermoplastic resin Resin which melts or softens when heated but re-hardens on cooling without chemical change.

Thermosetting resin Synthetic resin that undergoes irreversible chemical and physical changes when it is cured – a process accelerated by heat. Widely used in adhesives.

Traversing Planing wood across the grain, usually at an angle of 45 or 90 degrees, to reduce the thickness as easily as possible.

Underframing Framing, usually comprising legs and stretcher rails, supporting a chair seat, table or cabinet.

Wandering heart Log in which the heart or pith takes a crooked path, so that the saw crosses it in several places during conversion. The resulting timber is short-grained and difficult to work.

Wedging Method used in conjunction with mortise and tenon joints, whereby saw kerfs are made in the tenon and small wedges inserted so that they spread the tenon as it is driven home, thus greatly increasing the strength.

Whipping Tendency of a long thin rod or spindle to rotate unevenly while being turned in a lathe. It is controlled by using a special device called a 'steady'.

Winding Term applied to a frame or carcase which is twisted; it is also applied to boards. Pronounced to rhyme with 'kind'.

SUPPLIERS

HARDWARE AND KD FITTINGS

J. D. Beardmore & Co Ltd (Head Office)
Field End Road
Ruislip
Middlesex
HA4 0QG
Tel: 0181 804 6811
Shops at:
3–5 Percy Street, London W1P OEJ,
49 Park Street, Bristol,
120 Western Road, Hove, Sussex

General Woodwork Supplies
76–80 Stoke Newington High Street
London
N16 5BR
Tel: 0171 254 6052

Isaac Lord
Unit 5
Desborough Road Industrial Park
High Wycombe
Buckinghamshire
HP11 2QN
Tel: 01494 459191

Romany Tyzack
52–6 Camden High Street
London
NW1 0LT
Tel: 0171 3872579
The firm is part of the Tyzack Retail Group which has branches as follows:
Parker Tyzack at Catford, London; Parry Tyzack, Old Street, London and Borough High Street, London; Hall Tyzack at Merton (London), Bath, Bristol, Cardiff, Plymouth and Taunton.

Screwfix Direct
Freepost
Yeovil
Somerset
BA21 5YZ
Tel: 0800 317004

Woodfit Ltd
Ken Mill
Chorley
Lancashire
PR6 7EA
Tel: 01257 266421
Indispensable catalogue.

World of Wood
The Art Veneers Co Ltd
Industrial Estate
Mildenhall
Suffolk
IP28 7AY
Tel: 01638 712440
Very useful catalogue.

LEATHER TOPS AND LININGS

S. Doctors
5a Lansdown Mews
Farm Road
Hove
Sussex
Tel: 01273 774630

Dorn Antiques
Tew lane
Wooton
Woodstock
Oxfordshire
0X7 1HA
Tel: 01993 812023

World of Wood
(address as above)

WOOD FINISHES

Fiddes
Brindley Road
Cardiff
CF1 7TX
Tel: 01222 340323

Liberon Waxes Ltd
6 Park Street
Lydd
Kent
Tel: 01679 20107/21299
Waxes plus general polishing supplies; informative catalogue.

John Myland Ltd
80 Norwood High Street
London
SE27 9NW
Tel: 0181 670 9161
*Polishing materials, plus adhesives
and abrasives.*

Poth, Hille & Co Ltd
High Street
Stratford
London
E15 2QD
Tel: 0181 534 2291
*All kinds of waxes, especially rare
ones.*

Weaves and Waxes
53c Church Street
Bloxham
Banbury
Oxfordshire
OX15 4ET
Tel: 01295 721535

USEFUL CATALOGUES
Axminster Power Tool Centre
Chard Street
Axminster
Devon
EX13 5DZ
Tel: 01297 3436
*Hand tools; portable and standing
machines. Comprehensive range of
accessories rarely found elsewhere.
Catalogue free.*

John Boddy's Wood Store Ltd
Riverside Sawmills
Boroughbridge
North Yorkshire
Tel: 01423 322370
*Machinery, especially woodturning
lathes and their equipment. Wide
range of timbers including home-
grown and imported hardwoods.
Also a fascinating range of brasswork, decorative plaques and fittings for condiment grinders,
egg-timers etc. Catalogue £3,
refundable with first order.*

Rustin's Ltd
Waterloo Road
London
NW2 7TX
Tel: 0181 4504666
*All kinds of wood finishes, strip-
pers, restorers, oils etc. Catalogue
free.*

Screwfix Direct
Freepost
Yeovil
Somerset
BA21 5YZ
Tel: 00800 317004
*Every kind of fixing including KD
fittings, screws, bolts etc for wood-
workers, mechanics, electricians
and builders. Some portable tools;
also hardware and brasswork. Free
catalogue.*

**Trend Machinery & Cutting
Tools Ltd**
Penfold Works
Imperial Way
Watford
Hertfordshire
WD2 4YF
Tel: 01923 249911
*Every accessory and jig for your
router or for making your own
auxiliary equipment at home. Also
a wide range of cutters of all kinds,
and Trend's own saw blades for
sawbenches. Catalogue free.*

**Triton Workshop Systems
(UK) Ltd**
The Dale
Stoney Middleton
Hope Valley
Derbyshire
S32 4TF
Tel: 0800 856 7600
*Workcentres, router and jigsaw
tables, clamping systems. Cata-
logue and video free.*

INDEX